CW01649261

EINSTEIN AND THE ART OF SAILING

A NEW PERSPECTIVE ON THE ROLE OF LEADERSHIP

EINSTEIN AND THE ART OF SAILING

A NEW PERSPECTIVE ON THE ROLE OF LEADERSHIP

Anne de Graaf and Klaas Kunst

SHERWOOD PUBLISHING
• • • developing people

HERTFORD UK

Published by

Sherwood Publishing
Wildhill, Broadoak End, Hertford SG14 2JA, UK

www.sherwoodpublishing.com
email: sherwood@adinternational.com

Published 2010

A catalogue record of this book is available from the British Library.

ISBN 978-1-907037-03-0

Printed by J F Print Ltd., Sparkford, Somerset.
Illustrations by Luuk Poorthuis

CONTENTS

ACKNOWLEDGEMENTS

All questions, tasks and directions of thought in this book are based on three mainstreams of thought about organisations. During our quest for an inspirational range of ideas and inspiring representatives, we came up with three conceptual models: Transactional Analysis, System & Communications Theory and Group Relations Theory. Three masters, who play a leading role in these trends, crossed our path time and again. They set a lot of organisations in motion with their ideas. A brief thank you to Julie, Flor and John.

Julie Hay 'translated' concepts from Transactional Analysis, which were developed by others in the field of psychotherapy, to the daily reality of companies and organisations TA became widely popular in the seventies through bestsellers like Games People Play, I'm OK, You're ok. Since then, TA has continued redefining itself and countless new concepts have been added. Julie Hay is leading here in her own creative style. Her TA approach is a powerful mix of scientifically respected theory in easy language and practical ideas about applications of this to daily work and life.

The language sensitivity, acumen and relativisation by Flor Peeters, psychotherapist, staff member and educator at the Interactie Academy in Antwerp, made it clear to us that we live and work in a language reality. Since you cannot step away from your own language, there are limits on your ability to understand the other person. You can only understand yourself as someone who is trying to understand someone else. At the Interactie Academy, people look for possible answers to questions like: "What influences within the system affect the burden people experience, and how can this burden be made bearable and feasible"? These are questions about how a new perspective can come about in situations where people experience difficulty.

We are thankful for the wisdom of John Bazalgette from The Grubb Institute in London. He introduced us to Group Relations Theory. He taught us to "look below the surface." What can you extract from what you observe? What is the conflict really about deep down? The Grubb Institute teaches people in organisations and companies to take up the role of examiner. In this role it helps to keep asking questions! That is something that is important for everyone who knows that there is always more than meets the eye.

This book was made possible because many people we met during our consulting, education and training work were willing to share their ideas and experiences with us. We are deeply grateful to them. We also thank Ria van Elten, a key player in BMC Academy's back office, who has been our most loyal supporter for over 15 years.

Anne de Graaf and Klaas Kunst

We thank Stephen B. Karpman for permission to reproduce the diagram of the drama triangle in a style to suit this book: original diagram © 1967-2008 Stephen B. Karpman, M.D.

There are several questionnaires in this book. They were designed by Julie Hay and are printed here with permission for your personal use. They are copyrighted items and may not be reproduced. Copies are available for purchase at www.sherwoodpublishing.com

TO START WITH...

The title of this book refers to the famous work Zen and the art of motorcycle maintenance (Robert Pirsig, 1974). That book is no more about Zen Buddhism or engine maintenance, than ours is about Albert Einstein's theory of relativity; and it has absolutely nothing to do with the actual art of sailing a boat or ship. So, why did we choose this title?

Albert Einstein (1879-1955), one of the best known scientists of all time, became famous through his theory of relativity. He had the gift to examine the presuppositions of an entire culture. The consequences are overwhelming. Not only science, but also politics, literature, music, art, economy, psychology and morals underwent a revolution: a true iconoclasm. You can get to know his point of view on a number of matters by logging onto the website mentioned throughout this book (www.alberteinstein.nl).

Einstein was truly inspirational and a great spiritual leader. There are a lot of stories about him in circulation. The following anecdote teaches us something about Einstein's first steps towards winning the Nobel Prize. When a journalist asked him how he became such an incredible scholar, he responded that he had his mother to thank for that. Whenever he returned home from school, his mother always asked: "And, Albert, did you ask a good question today?" He often added: "I am not that smart, but I have learned to be genuinely curious and to ask questions." Whoever mirrors the methods of the most famous scholar of the 20th century can expect such an attitude to lead to new insights and wisdom. The subtitle of Pirsig's book states: "An inquiry into values." We apply a number of fundamental values in the life and work of managers in this book. Every question asked out of curiosity can be the beginning of something new.

In our role of consultant, trainer and coach we have worked together intensively with a lot of managers in many organisations in the public sector. We noticed that many organisations regularly found themselves in troubled waters and in bad weather. It is an art to maintain course or to set out a new course at the right time. Good leaders can do that. They use two forces, just like a sailor: their own force or power, and the power of the system. This is what we refer to as "the art of sailing." A good sailor knows the ecological system and makes optimum use of all the elements. A good sailor allows the wind and the streams to do their work where possible. At the same time, a good sailor uses their own insight, skills and power to maintain the rudder and the sail in the best possible position. If necessary, a good sailor dares to sail against the currents. Just as the sailor keeps the boat on course, the manager uses their personal knowledge and skills to maintain the ship of the organisation on course, and to weather any difficult times that cross its path.

This book is an invitation to managers to be curious and to ask questions, to be patient with questions that do not (yet) have answers, so that the answers (apparently!) can unfold on their own. These are questions about how you, your team, department and organisation function. The challenge does not lie so much in finding new answers, but in asking new questions. You will not know what you don't ask. You will not know what is not applied. We wish you lots of reading pleasure and... a pleasant struggle. One thing is crystal clear to us: the difference between a good manager and a bad one has nothing to do with the mistakes they make, but in how they deal with those mistakes.

Anne de Graaf is a training manager with BMC Academy and is an internationally accredited trainer and supervisor in organisational applications of Transactional Analysis.

Klaas Kunst is a director of the BMC Group and is certified in Systems and Communications Theory.

BMC Consultancy and Management is leading in consultancy for the Dutch public sector. With its approximately 2000 consultants BMC covers all the fields of the public sector, at central, local and regional level. BMC offers its widespread expertise to serve authorities in all countries, searching for modes to improve the quality of their public sector.

INTRODUCTION TO THE CORE CONCEPTS : HOW THIS BOOK IS STRUCTURED

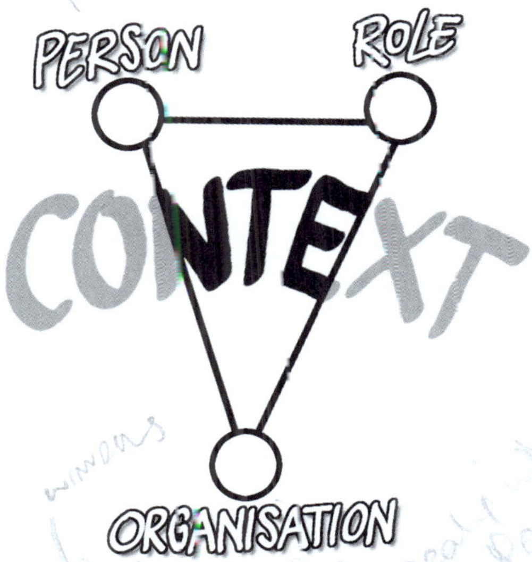

MAINSTREAM: THE QUALITIES OF A MODERN LEADER

The mainstreams together form the core of this book. These are representations of three central concepts: leadership, asking questions and the 'role' concept. Leadership is this book's main theme, asking questions – as Einstein would have done – looks at the investigative attitude of the manager and the role is the grail which the leader is constantly looking for.

MIRRORS: REFLECTIONS OF THE PERSON YOU ARE

The mirror is the metaphor for the reflection. You look at yourself in a mirror. You can reflect on what you can see in yourself. What is going well, what could be done better? In the reflection you will be given answers to questions like 'How do I see myself?', 'How do I come across?', 'What affects me?' and 'What is my dream where work is concerned?' And also: 'How can I turn this dream into reality?', 'Which laws and practical objections are in my way?'. You don't need to be ill in order to get better! The better you know yourself, the more you will realise where your strengths and opportunities can be found. Insight will help you to become the architect of your future.

WINDOWS: PERSPECTIVES OF THE SYSTEM WITHIN WHICH YOU WORK

The window is the metaphor for the view, the perspective, the way in which you can look at your organisation's reality. All windows provide a different view, one even more surprising and insight providing than the next. Every window offers a different perspective of reality. The windows will allow you to see the differences between people. These differences are unmistakably realistic and the question is therefore how you can deal with these differences. Windows can offer new perspectives of the organisation within which you work.

DIRECTIONS OF THOUGHT: TEMPORARY ANSWERS TO DIFFICULT QUESTIONS

Every direction of thought provokes thoughts, invites people to think along in a specific direction. A thought trail helps with the search for temporary answers to sometimes difficult questions. A thought trail doesn't offer complete summaries or realities. The trail literally wants to provoke thoughts – no more and no less. After all, the question isn't 'what is reality?', but 'how are we going to look at reality?'.

WHAT REALLY MATTERS TO YOU!

HOW CAN YOU GET THE VERY MOST OUT OF THIS BOOK?

Years ago we followed a multiple day training course in London. We tried our best to get to grips with the material and to apply this in practical situations together with colleagues from right across Europe. Making notes, practising, exchanging, reading. The final session turned out to be unforgettable. The Institute Director addressed the group and recommended that we "forget everything we had learned". Some hilarity arose amongst the participants, but certainly also some unrest. Reacting to the confusion, he added: "because what really matters you truly can't forget!"

The core of real learning is all about things which truly matter to you. This isn't something you can just simply forget, even if you wanted to. Frenetic studying and really learning something are mutually exclusive. Less studying and more learning! This is exactly how you can deal with this book and your own learning process too. It may seem like you have forgotten a great deal after you have read it. Then ask yourself what really mattered to you. You will definitely not lose sight of this. However, there are things you can do to get as much as possible out of reading this book. You can achieve even more with the following suggestions

1. Often tell others about what you have learnt.
   - Explain what you have learnt to your friends and colleagues.
   - You remember 20% of what you hear, 40% of what you read and 80% of what you explain to others.

2. Make use of the momentum.
   - Immediately start carrying out the intentions and decisions you reached when you were reading. Make a flying start with the execution of your plan.
   - If you consistently apply something for 30 days, it will become part of your normal routine.

3. Regularly read through your assignment answers.
   - Go through them every day the week after you have finished the book, weekly a month after reading and monthly during the year which follows.
   - You will retain 80% of the information if you do this; if not, only 15% will remain.

4. Produce a plan in your agenda with all the aspects from the book which you are definitely going to apply.
   - Organise these across a period of time, ensuring you have a specific area of attention or assignment every day.
   - If you want to apply everything you have learnt straight away, then the likelihood is nothing much will come of it. Give yourself some time!

5. Read books which are directly linked to the subject of your specific interest.
   - Do this for an hour every day: the literature list can provide some assistance in this regard.
   - If you have knowledge of concepts, then this will enable you to organise (new) information more effectively and generalise (new) insights to other situations more easily.

MAINSTREAM

QUALITIES OF A MODERN LEADER

MAINSTREAM 1 THE TASK OF A LEADER

After having taught for years in the monastery, the monk visited his student. "There is one more issue you have to resolve before your training is complete," he said. "There was once a family who owned a chick. The chick lived in a round pot and was cared for lovingly. After a while, the chick had almost finished growing into an adult chicken. Meanwhile, he was fully wedged in the pot and couldn't move at all. The question to you is: How does the chick come out of the pot?" The monk returned to his quarters, which were strictly off limits to his students. The student was all alone with the issue of "the chick in the pot." He thought deeply about the issue and concentrated fully on the development of chicks. He devoured every piece of literature on all sorts and sizes of pots, and debated the issue with other students. Worried, he roamed the halls of the student home: "Chick! Pot? Pot! Chick?" He started getting more and more anxious. The more he studied, the more frustrated he became. Then he got up and did the one thing that had been strictly forbidden. He hurried to the monk's quarters, banged on the door, stormed inside and shouted: "To hell with the chick! To hell with the pot. The monk gazed at him kindly as if he had expected him and said: "Aha, the chicken is finally out of the pot!"

KICK-OFF

The monk had understood. His task was to create "his equal". The student finally understood it too: to become a real monk, he had to cross the boundaries that were set for the student. You have to have courage to be a leader, but you also have to have courage to become one. This is a typical dilemma surrounding leadership. It takes guts to be a leader and to take the lead. Bad leaders create followers; good leaders create leaders! Leadership is enabling your organisation, your department or your team to achieve the desired objectives. The leader facilitates the learning and development process, asks questions and creates a bond. He puts the learnings into practice and at the same time, he asks questions that arise from practice. The many changes of these times have a significant impact on leadership. It is no longer the king on his throne or the admiral on his ship, but instead it is the facilitator who plays a key role.

Bad leaders create followers; good leaders create leaders

Assumption: Leadership in healthy organisations is not only reserved for the hierarchical leader(s). The increasing complexity of the organisations themselves and their "outside world" make it less and less possible to know everything about everything (see also Direction of Thought 1). Avoid: knowing everything better, or even, knowing it better than anyone else.

Now, more than ever, formal management must want, be able and dare to trust the power of good employees. Therefore, recruiting is crucial! Whoever makes a good selection "at the door" will also dare to give more space to employee leadership. If this is not the case, something has gone wrong at the beginning. It all boils down to recruiting or training employees who deliver top quality and are allowed and dare to lead in certain areas. Everyone can show leadership anywhere in the organisation. The more people there are who show leadership, the less the organisation has to depend on formal managers. Individual competencies gain an important added value if they also complement and unite the organisation.

In the old paradigm, leadership was practically equal to a position "high up on the corporate ladder" at the top of the pyramid.

In the new leadership paradigm, we think chiefly in terms of a matrix. Everyone can display leadership, be authoritative and take charge at a crossroads, somewhere in the organisation. That does not take place as "force and power" but primarily as "authority and flexibility". Leaders are not only heard because they are the boss, but because they are leaders in certain areas and they set an example. Formal management can stimulate this tremendously and make maximum use of the qualities of the employees. Even the formal leaders from the pyramid take on positions at crossroads and are authoritative in the eyes of others.

Clarity about roles and the related authority ensure that there are also clear boundaries in the matrix about who makes decisions about what.

A successful manager is often called a born leader. The American psychologist, Carl Rogers, even asserted that you should not train managers, you just have to select them. The qualities that employees ascribe to managers that inspire them have mainly to do with the personalities of those managers. What managers do is primarily determined by *the roles* they take. How they do it is mainly determined *by the person* they are. This aspect is decisive for success!

It is great if you naturally possess all sorts of leadership qualities. However, it is more complex than "you have it" or "you don't have it." The existence of the so-called born leader can also be a myth and can stand in the way of leadership development in organisations. Not everything has to be innate: you can also learn a lot through education and training!

QUESTION

What have you learned recently?

Leadership is an inside job. Developing the leadership role comes from the inside – not only from your head, but especially from your heart and soul. A modern leader creates a place where people prosper, so they can contribute even more to the joint task ahead of them. The most important tool is your communications skill that consists of more than just talking. It is an illusion to think that all questions will be answered if you use the right words and form the right sentences. With the words you use, you only describe a certain world, the world you create with your own words!

TASK

A director of an educational institution once said that learning is only what you never forget. You don't forget it because it is communicated to you at the right time, by the right person using the right tone. Most of what you have learned, you didn't learn at school or in a college classroom. Everyday practice is the best school. There is a teacher and a student for everyone in every organisation. It is encouraging to realise that you learn lessons from inspiring people around you, and that you can inspire others who can learn important lessons from you. You don't usually forget the "teacher" who taught you what you never forgot.

1. Think about someone who is or has been a leader at work or in your life. Someone who was so inspirational that you would not forget them very quickly. This person can be a teacher from school, a guide from your trainee period, or perhaps someone whom you met at your first job. You probably still remember the person's name?

The person who inspired me =

2. What did (or does) this leader do that makes you think back with happy memories? Do you still remember the exact moments that you felt a spark fly? What were you doing at that moment that was so important to you?
3. What was it that had such an impact on you? Can you use a few catchwords that express the core of what inspired you?
4. If you look at these words again more closely, can you point out a main word or a core term that connects these words together?

DIRECTION OF THOUGHT 1: LEADERSHIP, BUT DIFFERENT

Our society is changing at lightning speed. Doing today what worked yesterday often results in less effectiveness. This century apparently requires different leadership than last century. Five changes portrayed in the drawings illustrate this.

- Last century's leaders could get by with maintaining the organisation's product offerings at the same level. In this century, customer demands seem to form the basis for establishing business processes.

What did you do in the past few months to manage customer-oriented employees in a customer-oriented manner?

- Yesterday's leaders possessed the information and knowledge to perform the necessary duties. Many modern organisations now depend largely on knowledge workers and are characterised by a knowledge democracy.

What have you noticed that indicates knowledge is no longer powerful in your organisation?

- In the past, employees stayed with a company or organisation their whole lives Mobility has increased tremendously. New employees sometimes enter the organisation and announce they will stay only until there is nothing more to learn.

What did you do during this past week to create involvement and a bond?

- Managers used to have the necessary resources. Assigning and monitoring those resources was one of their main duties. Today's complexity puts many resources beyond their control.

How can you be responsible for things that you have no control over?

How do you stay in charge?

New employees sometimes enter the organisation and announce they will only stay until there is nothing more to learn

- In the days when the future looked a lot like the past, managers used their experience to prove their worth in decision making processes. Now that the future no longer resembles the past in any way, shape or form, the importance of experience seems to be a less decisive factor.

How do you, as a manager, make sure your employees keep learning and exploring?

Many managers discover they can no longer do their job based solely on their rank in the hierarchy. Looking at the differences between old and new organisations, three things stand out, which are portrayed again in sketches:

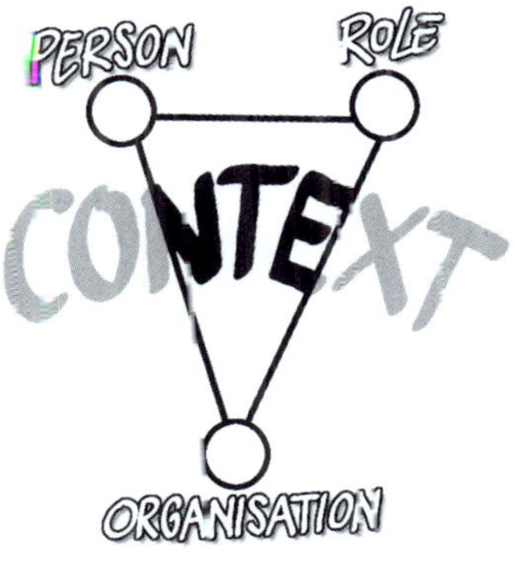

1. People view the organisation differently nowadays. The old organisation functioned like a machine: routine, efficient and predictable. The modern organisation is becoming its own universe, where everything is connected to everything else. It has become a network of enterprising people who are always learning new things.
2. Managers who view themselves with an open mind have a better effect on others. The personality of the manager highly influences the achievement of success. As a manager, a part of you is always involved in that success! Knowing who you are, what you can contribute, what you know (and don't know) – in short, a healthy sense of self reflection – characterises the leader of today.
3. Other views are evolving about the role of the manager. Delegating and monitoring tasks used to be a manager's main job in the past. Today's world requires inspirational and motivational leaders. Leaders who do not necessarily want to be in the limelight, but leaders who step aside and give others the opportunity to take the ball and run with it to be successful.

Leadership can be defined in many different ways. But not a single one of those definitions truly explains the dynamics and the complexity of leadership. A Scottish saying best describes the essence of leadership "To show the way by going first!" It's a combination of setting the example and having (entrepreneurial) courage. Employees don't do what you say, they look at what you do. Make sure your ego is not what motivates you; let an inspiring vision be your guide.

A hungry traveller arrived at a very poor village. He understood he couldn't just beg for food. He proposed to the villagers to cook a large pot of soup. Imagine how surprised they were; they hadn't eaten any soup in a very long time! But the traveller contended that he had everything he needed in his backpack. A big pot of water would be all he needed. He pulled a large stone out of his backpack. "This is not a regular stone," he said when he saw their questioning faces: "This is a real soup stone!" He placed the stone in the water. Everyone waited in anticipation, full of curiosity. "The soup needs some seasoning," he said after a while. Luckily, someone had some salt at home; a neighbour also had a couple of bay leaves. A little while later the traveller said: "The soup needs a little cooking oil." Another person then remembered that he had some meat for the soup in the cellar. The same man said, "It should be a little creamier," since he saw a potato plant in the garden. The potatoes were added to the soup. "How about some carrots?" someone asked suddenly. Another person remembered he had a couple of turnips. Someone else came with some leeks, and the neighbour down the road had some beans… It didn't take long before the whole house was filled with a wonderful aroma. The traveller departed gratefully. "You can keep the soup stone," he said, "You can use it to cook more soup whenever you want." After he left, the villagers said: "What a magical stone." Once the villagers could no longer see him, the traveller picked up another stone and put it in his backpack.

QUESTION

What three qualities do you possess to inspire and motivate your employees?

DIRECTION OF THOUGHT 2: MANAGING TEAMWORK

Eighty percent of all plane crashes are caused by pilot error that could have been prevented if the cockpit crew had worked together better as a team. Thus, pilot training has been focusing more on teamwork, open communication, direct feedback, listening to one another and saying what you think.

Organisations can also crash. Many organisations could have been "saved from their demise" if those in charge had worked together better as a team. The frequent change in coaches, as is common practice in the world of sports, would lead us to believe that the coach is all-powerful. Replacing the coach does not guarantee better results: it is often more complex than that. Likewise, the management team of an organisation will not necessarily "play better ball" if you replace the CEO. The most successful organisations are characterised by a management team comprised of many different personalities who have the great desire to provide a contribution together as a team. Complementing competencies make all the difference in the world! These organisations have managers who are capable of leading this collaborative team. They possess the art of aligning the organisational objectives with the many qualities of the employees.

"Managing teamwork" sounds like a contradiction in terms. You either provide a path and manage it by motivating your employees to follow that path, or you work together as a team and you determine the path together, assigning tasks in collaboration with everyone. Nevertheless, successful managers do not see any contradiction here. The trick is to go beyond this contradiction. Managing teamwork is a first-rate management skill. A collaborative "crew" is necessary to prevent your organisation from having to "abort take-off", "make an emergency landing" or "crash". The top priorities of a manager are to create a first-rate team, manage the (communications) process and maintain goal-oriented teamwork. The main goal is a safe flight for everyone! As many companies are reorganising and moving the responsibility more towards the heart of the organisation, closer to the workfloor, the question "Who will manage the teamwork?" is becoming vitally important.

Replacing the coach does not guarantee better results

Managing a group of employees, working together as a team with a lot of responsibility, requires a huge investment in building the team. The individual team members have all sorts of wants and needs. First of all, they want to feel safe. A safe haven makes it easier and more appealing to contribute. Then it will be possible to develop the desire to influence outcomes, which will automatically result in the need to work together as a team. This, in turn, leads to the desired added value of the team.

This succession is not linear but cyclical in nature.

SAFETY (S) → INFLUENCE (I) → TEAMWORK (T)

Safety (S)

The most basic need of individuals in a group is the need for safety. If the group climate is unsafe, people will create their own individual safety. Some people will withdraw while others will become overactive.

Colleague Wilson asks for the floor at a meeting to contribute to a discussion about an important policy. He is tense because he does not generally expose himself so easily and these tigers around the table make him feel like easy prey. Some of his colleagues make it clear, verbally and non-verbally, that they are not really interested in his input. People are laughing at him and his manager is chuckling along with the rest of the room. Is it any wonder that Wilson, a municipality housing specialist, decides right then-and-there to never speak up again? After this experience, he resorted to only communicating "safely" via e-mail and memorandums.

In a team where it is not safe enough to "say what is on your mind", team members will start grumbling on the sidelines. People will (still) discuss matters in the hallways that cannot be verbalised on the work floor. The task of the manager is to create an atmosphere in which everyone can feel safe. Only then can team members take advantage of one another's contributions. This will have a positive effect on the effectiveness and the productivity of the team!

TASK

Without fully realising it, you probably do a lot to create a safe workplace for your employees, a place that encourages employees to influence others. Can you provide examples? What is most important to you? What can wait a while?

Influence (I)

If the coast is clear, people will meet their need to exercise their influence. Nothing is as frustrating as not being able to make your own (unique) contribution. Fundamentally, everyone wants to use their qualities to help achieve good results. However, that means that their input must be seen, heard and valued by others. If a person is losing their "sense of influence" they will lose their sense of involvement and will often switch over to "automatic pilot". A team (leaders and members) that wants to excel must provide a climate in which everyone's personal and professional qualities are valued!

Teamwork (T)

If it is safe (enough), if everyone's input is recognised, if obstacles can be overcome, teamwork appears to work all by itself. This is also essential, because teamwork is a necessary inconvenience with no alternative. Inconvenient, because it's not always easy to work with others. Misunderstandings and miscommunications are lurking in every corner and you have to wait and see if the result is successful. However, there is often no alternative to teamwork. After all, you can't be a hospital, a school or a government organisation, a family or a volleyball team all by yourself.

To co-operate is a challenge with no alternative

Teamwork can only flourish in a safe and trusting environment. A good leader will invest in it. A foundation for safety is formed by the area where people exert influence. Only then can people put forth their best qualities. Safety and influence create the necessary atmosphere for teamwork. It is about each individual's needs in a team: the student in a classroom, the government official in a department meeting, the nurse in a team meeting, the manager in a progress meeting. This is the best recipe for productive teamwork.

DIRECTION OF THOUGHT 3: BOUNDARIES AND OPPORTUNITIES

TASK

In the previous task you named three qualities you use to inspire and motivate your employees. How did you find out you possessed these qualities?

It is so easy to say that each person is unique. But if you, we and they are really that unique, there will be a lot of tension that cannot be resolved. This tension is due to the impossibility of being able to understand one another completely. Unicity is a term that means that everyone is unique in how they give meaning to the things that happen to them. This makes people less accessible to each other. Your first reaction is that you can assume another person understands you and you understand the other person. However, if you consider the uniqueness of each person, it is more likely that complicated misunderstandings will easily occur during communication. Our language is a tool to understand each other, but verbal communication is a very limited option. You have to be able to listen to one another very well if you want to hear half of what is being said. Language is, as it were, an 'approximate-indication'.

A director or manager views the organisation differently than do other employees. It has little to do with hierarchy; it has more to do with a different point of view or standpoint. Each position gives you a different point of view; you see things differently and reality has a different meaning depending on your perspective. This is what makes reality so complex. These differences are a fact and will remain so. They cannot be resolved. The real question is how you handle these differences and how you make them work.

Language is an approximate-indication

When the Israelites stood face to face with the giant Goliath for the very first time, their reaction was: "He is enormous! We will never be able to defeat him!" When David thought about it again, he thought: "He is so huge, I will hit him every time!"

When recognising these different perspectives, you might wonder what is true and what is not. The idea that there is only one truth appears to be outdated. What can be considered as a truth and what cannot only exists and moves within the communication between people.

This means that communication is always a negotiation, not about what is true, but about how the truth can be viewed. People find a direction for their thoughts and actions while in dialogue with one another. This actually turns individuals into "interpeople": What we view as reality is found between people, not in people. How do you as a manager shape the necessary dialogue? In a quest for efficiency, dialogue took on the form of meetings since the beginning of the last century. But all those meetings have focused unilaterally on the formal side. The efficiency gained from this was lost to adjusting and fine-tuning. Business-like, systematic and routine meetings have not led to the desired effective communication and transparent decision making. Other forms of communication and interaction are (also) necessary. The casual and informal contact: speaking the same language, the apparent, illogical reasoning of skipping from one subject to another, the solidifying conversation – these are all ways to be better attuned to the environment through communication, to test one's own directions of thought, and to discover how one's thoughts match with other people's thoughts.

In a quest for efficiency, dialogue took on the form of a meeting

You influence others and others influence you. It's chitchat. This chitchat is no unnecessary luxury; it's an absolute necessity and is as much a part of life as walking, eating, drinking and playing. It's also never without engagement! Each conversation does something to you; it touches you and influences you. Deliberate chitchat also offers new opportunities for managers to keep the dialogue going with their employees, to exercise influence differently than in a formal setting. Chitchat helps you to better understand; it reinforces the feeling of having a connection and gives meaning to the efforts put forth at work (and thus also in life). Chitchat is not always about *something*, but it is always about *us*. Casual conversation and informal meetings are necessary to know who you are (in the other person's eyes and in your own eyes) and where you stand (as perceived by others and by you). The realisation that you are good at something arises from the communicative exchange and examination with others. This can also be proved from the task at the beginning of this chapter. You discover your qualities through the responses of others.

TASK

How do you as a manager provide room, perhaps without realising it, for casual contact, for a spontaneous conversation, for chitchat?

How do you think you can provide better direction and room for this spontaneity?

As a leader, you can expect the following:

- You can only understand and be understood to a limited degree.
- You will disappoint people, put them at a disadvantage and sometimes hurt them.
- You will create misunderstandings unintentionally.
- Your words will not be enough.
- Your meetings will not be so efficient.

This list is not meant to discourage you. It is meant to put the manager's ego back into the right proportions; it teaches perspective, leads to more attention, requires more creativity and makes the ultimate appeal to your thinking abilities. What can you do? The most important thing you can do is to keep the dialogue flowing, and to shape and lead the discourse and agreements about interpretations. Lead the negotiations about how people can view the future. Allow everyone's personal struggle with their own role within the system they are a part of.

Your employees will test to see if their direction of thought is correct through their contact with you as their manager and in their encounters with each other. This offers you opportunities for influence, encouragement, creating perspective, support, shading, nuance and quality questions. The manager who casually skips this process creates lonely and misunderstood employees who will feel even more demotivated in their quest to be heard and understood. In the end, you, the manager, will see them as difficult, unmotivated or disloyal. This opinion would be a cheap shot ("That Brown bloke, you can't work with him!") and it would not improve the situation at all. And, if you think your employees might be difficult, unmotivated or disloyal, you must be communicating that in one way or another, and they will notice it. The escalation of mutual misunderstanding will only increase and the efficiency you dreamt of will be destroyed.

DIRECTION OF THOUGHT 4: WINDOWS ON THE ORGANISATION

It makes a lot of difference which window you choose when looking at your organisation. The perspective determines and limits your observation! The traditional focus of managing requires an adjustment. Always coming up with new rules and structures, tools and policies will not lead to the desired solution. People have been looking through the organisation-oriented window too much for too long. The 21st century invites innovation: a more environment-oriented, results-oriented and people-oriented way of doing business. This requires the manager to have the courage to look through a different window.

There is a movement underway in organisational development to change from hard to soft and from internal to external. The focus on the people-oriented side of organisation is growing, as is the attention to the environment in which the organisation operates. There is also more attention given to the results to be achieved, which is essential. In the (future) role of leadership you can use four windows on the organisation to differentiate between roles.

Window 1 The organisation-oriented window

Managers have always liked to look through the organisation-oriented window a lot. There is nothing wrong with that. In the best case scenario, you will see a well-oiled machine running its fixed process routines with clearly established responsibilities. The manager clearly specifies what has to happen and the employees know what they have to do. Control and regulate is the central theme.

Window 2 The people-oriented window

Looking through the people-oriented window gives you a different picture of the organisation. The behaviour of people comes more into focus. The culture of the organisation (culture = behaviour!) is viewed as an important success and failure factor for the organisation's results. If you look closely, you will see through this window how the involvement and efforts of employees increase through participation. You will see the leader motivating and bringing people together.

Window 3 The environment-oriented window

The person who looks through the environment-oriented window sees how the organisation anticipates what is taking place contextually. Customer-oriented and demand-driven informational impulses from the environment determine what products and services are to be prepared. Schools, hospitals, public and private sector organisations and institutions emphatically focus on the demands and needs from the environment. Employees are busy with discovery and innovation.

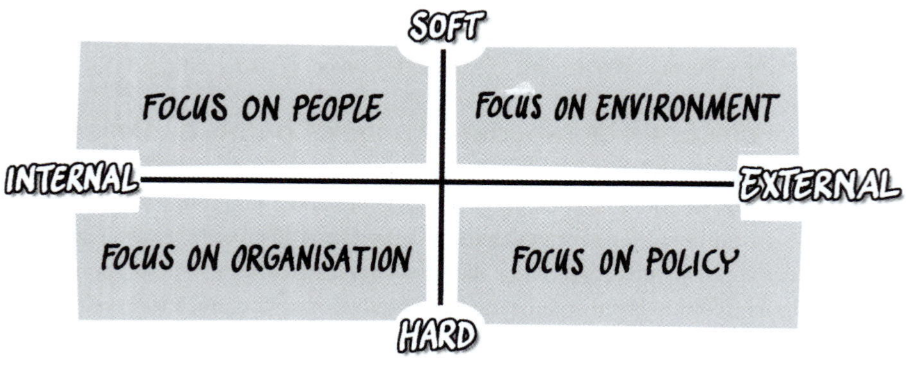

Window 4 The results-oriented window

This window focuses on the drive in the organisation to formulate policy objectives and to achieve these objectives in production and service. Employees are inspired by social tasks. They want to achieve good results with students! They want to deliver customised care! They want to deliver adequate documents quickly! A lot of time and energy are put into determining the path and in performance.

Many managers have been made blind to the real business by unilaterally looking through a single window. Single-mindedness can cause serious damage to an organisation. The custom to look chiefly through the organisational window has contributed to the fact that managers can no longer see clearly through the other windows. They look through them in a haze of maintaining and managing in their minds. Thus many options for useful interventions have completely gone out of the window. This impedes real innovation. Managers say they are working on being people-oriented, but they have mutilated that into a management tool that is referred to as competency management. Managers say they want to be results-oriented, but that is packaged in all sorts of planning and control rituals. Managers say they are working in an environmentally-oriented manner, but they come up with organisational-oriented structures and tooling requirements that lead to more overheads.

They say they want to be results-oriented, but they have packaged that into all sorts of planning & control rituals

Take a look through a different window! Let yourself be surprised by what you see and by the treasure of opportunities that come into view. The following task will put you on the right path.

TASK

It's not what you say, it's what you do that demonstrates through which window you prefer to look at your organisation. Below are a number of activities that managers spend their time and energy on.

1. Choose the three you think you spend most of your time and energy on:
   - I keep up with what is going on in the world surrounding my organisation. (explore)
   - I make sure my organisation is always renewing itself! (renew)
   - I encourage my people to learn and grow! (motivate)
   - I succeed in having my people work well together! (bring together)
   - I know what takes place in my organisation is essential! (govern)

- I arrange for people in my organisation to do what they have to do! (arrange)
- I make sure everyone is on the same page in my organisation! (determine the course)
- I succeed in having people perform at optimum levels in my organisation! (perform)

2. Discuss your choice with one or more of your employees. Ask for their feedback!
3. Ask your employees which activities they think you should spend more time on in the future. Have them explain why!
4. Make a plan for improvement or change if you wish. Always involve the employees.

... AND THE ART OF SURFING

You can enter the website www.alberteinstein.nl. You can choose the English version. There you will find an in-depth test about "connective leadership'. Complete the questionnaire to gain a clear picture of what kind of manager you are. Based on the results, you can decide what areas you would like to develop.

MAINSTREAM 2 BETTER QUESTIONS LEAD TO BETTER ANSWERS

When a journalist asked Einstein how he became such a scholar, Einstein answered that he had his mother to thank for that. After being asked more questions, he explained that when he came home from school, his mother always asked: "And Albert, did you ask a good question today?" The scholar often added to this story: "I am not so bright, I am just particularly curious!"

KICK OFF

By asking good questions you will automatically enter into a dialogue with the people around you. You really need the people around you to help you form your own viewpoints and opinions. You cannot know if you are on the right track all by yourself. You need other people. By working as a manager, you will discover that dialogue will take you further than discussion. Dialogue enables the free exchange of perspectives, whereby the dialogue partners take note of their mutual differences and look for the synthesis of these differences. Dialogue enables the flow of meanings and has an open, equal and social character. Dialogue means: both people talking, conversation, exchange of ideas. The Greek word "dialogos" literally means: meaning that flows through something. The word "debate" literally means: knock down. "Discussion" has the same linguistic background as percussion ("knocking apart"). The experience with debates and discussions shows that the parties mainly look for arguments for their own (!) point of view. In this way, they dig themselves deeper and deeper into the trench of their own opinions. So deep that a person can no longer recognise that the other person might be right, or that the other person at least has a valuable point of view. An opinion is not much more than a subjective meaning given to a selective observation. People tend to launch their opinions against each other in debates and discussions ('Yes, but...'), whereas in a dialogue, people tend to think things through together ('Yes, and...'). If everyone calls out in a discussion "look at me" and "listen to me", they will lose sight of each other and none of them will be heard. The chance they will learn something from each other is next to nothing. Dialogue or discussion, flow or strike, that's the question!

A meaning is not much more than giving a subjective meaning to a selective observation

TASK

Think of the questions you ask yourself about how you manage others. You always have these questions with you without realising it. The art is to learn to listen to them and to make them explicit. If you are consciously aware of the question, an answer is not very far away. Can you name three such questions?

DIRECTION OF THOUGHT 1: ASK QUESTIONS

The main purpose of meetings between manager and employee is to increase an employee's problem solving skills and autonomy. If the meeting does not contribute to that goal, for example because the manager constantly proposes solutions, the employee will become more dependent. The consequence is that they will take less initiative and responsibility and will start showing reactive and passive behaviour. Asking questions activates an employee's thinking process, makes them active and responsible for their own solutions and options. Thinking is often expressing thoughts about things that have already been thought up in the past. Thinking is given a chance if you ask an open question, which is followed by silence. If it is silent for a brief period, or if someone looks up at the ceiling, you are apparently on the right path or direction (of thought).

The goal of meetings is to increase an employee's problem solving skills

To keep meetings with employees results-oriented, it is useful to recognise the different phases of a meeting. Goal-oriented meetings have the following three phases in common:

- Issue
- Goal
- Action.

Sandra heads up a large department at a Water Authority. Her director regularly conducts meetings with her regarding the progress of her work. During the meetings, Sandra examines and discovers the issues that are currently relevant at work. Sandra worries about questions like:

1. How is it possible that the performance agreements will not be achieved by my department this past half year?
2. What opportunities might I have missed when communicating with my department?

The meeting between the director of the Water Authority and the head of the department, Sandra, starts out with questions and answers (!) to examine and clarify the issue. This does not always involve a life or death problem. All questions, issues and problems that are relevant to the work situation can become a subject of discussion.

- "What do you worry about most when you think about the results up until now"?
- "What do you think is going well at this time and what improvements can be made in your department"?
- "Explain how you think your project is progressing"?

If the issues have been examined sufficiently (asking questions seems to be the most effective method), the goal that Sandra wants to achieve will be explored. The following are examples:

- "I want to understand better why I am so over-sensitive when I meet with Giles"!
- "My goal for this meeting is to gain new ideas for a different approach."
- "My goal is to involve my colleagues more in the preparations for the project."

Attention can be focused on developing new perspectives and clear objectives. Finally, action agreements are made and implemented.

- "I am going to write a plan and discuss it with you in the coming month."
- "I am going to talk to Giles about my difficulty in making good work agreements with him."
- "I will start the weekly project team meetings with a round of "what is going well and what needs improvement"?

The following points remain important:

- The employee considers themself (co-) responsible for the progress.
- The manager helps the employee to gain insight.
- Each next phase can only be successful if the previous phase was also successful.

DIRECTION OF THOUGHT 2: SHAPES AND TYPES OF QUESTIONS

The meeting between the manager and the employee is first of all about clarifying the nature of the issue. Being able to ask questions is an essential skill. It is handy if you know how to ask the following types of questions:

- What? and How? questions
- Open questions
- Short, simple questions

What? and How? questions are often more effective than Why? questions. "Why is this report not finished yet?" Why did you let the class leave early?" "Why did you let the transfer get so out of hand?" Why? questions examine the reason for something; they inquire about the background. Providing clarity about behaviour – answering why? – is easer if the other person has more information about an issue. If the why? question has to be asked, it is better to ask it at the end of a conversation than at the beginning. Otherwise, the Why? question can make the person feel as though they are being blamed for something. The person can easily interpret the question as an accusation, for example: "Why didn't you do that sooner?" Most Why? questions are easy to convert into What? and How? questions. "How did it come about that you couldn't make the delivery earlier?

What do you think was the reason that it took so long?"

The term "open questions" suggests something about the desired effect. An open question leaves all possibilities open for the person with whom you are speaking. These types of questions motivate the other person to talk about what they are thinking and feeling. "How did this reach the stage it is at?" The answer is more or less predetermined when asking a closed question. "You are probably not happy with this situation?" "Don't you also think it's high time to intervene?"

Whoever asks a closed question will only receive an echo of their own view of the issue as an answer

These types of questions do not encourage anyone to tell their own story. Whoever asks a closed question will only receive an echo of their own view of the issue as an answer. 'Have you ever thought about contacting him?' A closed question! Besides, the suggestion is clear: "Contact him!" But: "What have you done until now to handle this issue?" Or: "What other options do you have?" These are open questions, which make the other person think.

TASKS

Change the following closed questions into new, open questions:

- Wouldn't you like to contact them?
- Wouldn't it be better to tell her the whole truth?
- Shall I tell you something?
- Are you suitable for this function?
- You probably think that is difficult, don't you?
- Was it a good meeting?
- You are probably here to ask me how to continue?
- You probably had a difficult childhood?

Keep the questions brief and simple. The answer to the question "Can I count on it or not? And how is what's-his-name?" are difficult to answer. These types of questions generate confusion. It is clearer to ask separate questions. Also so-called or/or questions are confusing. The other person is encouraged to choose between two alternatives, which may lead them to believe that there are no other options. “Are you going to discuss it with your team right away or are you first going to meet with a couple of project leaders?”

Reconsider the questions that you asked at the beginning of this chapter. Are they what? and how? questions? Are they open questions? Are they brief and simple? If not, change them into open questions! Can you see a better effect?

DIRECTION OF THOUGHT 3: ATTRIBUTION

If you consider all the questions that you actually ask, hopefully a lot of questions, are these questions about yourself or about others? If they are about you, and you are the subject of the question as it were, there is a better chance for change than if others are the subject of the question. You can see that in the word “I” in your question. If it is about “they” or “you”, you place the desired change outside of yourself. Of course you would like to see something change with the others, but you are the only key that fits! You can influence how you think, feel and what you do, not what others think, feel or do.

Research shows that people who mainly see the source of a problem situation being beyond themselves are very susceptible to symptoms of powerlessness and stress. They believe that the causes will be permanent and cannot be influenced by them. This is a so-called external attribution pattern. People with an internal attribution pattern first look at themselves to find the origin of their feelings of powerlessness and stress. They remain capable of seeing their own part and maintaining the power over their own actions. This allows them to maintain the feeling that they can exercise influence over a problem situation. This in turn minimises any stress they might experience.

Stephen Covey (1997) clearly differentiates between the “circle of influence” and the “circle of concern.” The circle of influence relates to things that you can do something about. There are many things you may be concerned about, but the question is what can you influence? You can feel concerned about a lot of things, but the (smaller) circle that you can influence is decisive! Interesting conversations about endless traffic jams, bad weather and management incompetence do very little for you, except wear you down. These types of conversations are mainly reactive and a waste of energy. However, you can be active inside your circle of influence; take responsibility and influence things. It costs energy, but it gives you a lot of new energy!

The will to understand! That's what it's all about in Einstein's vision. The challenge is not in finding new answers, but in asking new questions. Every improvement, every solution and all renewal and progress are preceded by asking new questions. It is worthwhile to want to improve existing things, from the will to improve. Are we doing the right things? Do we do the things we do well? The questions you ask determine the focus you create for yourself! Simply expressing a problem you have through complaining and arguing might make you feel better, but it doesn't solve anything. The questions you ask yourself determine what you are focusing on mentally. "How should I handle the split that is threatening my management team? What more can I do to increase my project team's results? What are the points that need work to speed up the process in my department?" Asking questions results in dynamics, and great questions invariably leads to dialogue! Thus, the way to change your focus and create more dynamics is to keep asking questions.

Are we doing the right things?
Are we doing the things we do well?

Children ask the best questions. They bombard their environment every day with their questions. Whoever listens to them carefully will see the world through different eyes. "Mum, why doesn't the moon fall down? Dad, what time do the people on the other side of the world go to bed? Why can't a caterpillar fly?" Children don't ask questions to aggravate adults; they ask questions because they are genuinely curious and they really want to understand something. Questions are the best tool to learn everything about life. All questions emanate from each person's search for the core question in life: What does someone like me do with someone like you in a world like ours? This is a question that can keep you busy for a lifetime! See Mirror 6.

"It is essential to not stop asking questions. Curiosity exists for a reason. You cannot do anything else but look in awe at the mysteries of this century, of life, of the fantastic structure of reality. It is enough if you try to understand just a little bit of the mystery every day. Don't ever lose your curiosity."

Albert Einstein.

DIRECTION OF THOUGHT 4: THE RIGHT QUESTIONS AT THE RIGHT TIME

If you don't ask a right question, there will be no right answer. It's more than just a conversation technique. The open, brief, what? or how? question generates the answer that really helps the asker. The "logical levels" model, developed by Robert Dilts, helps the manager ask questions that really help employees. The answers offer opportunities to take the issue a step further.

The skill of asking good questions is reserved for those who are good listeners. How do you know you are asking the right questions to help the other person explore and change their current situation? People go through a number of stages when solving issues. There are six levels; and each higher level contains or is influenced by all the lower levels.

If you don't ask a right question, you will not get a right answer

■ **Spirituality / purpose**	What makes my life worth living?
■ **Identity / Mission**	Who am I actually?
■ **Beliefs / Values**	Why am I doing this or that?
■ **Capabilities / Strategies**	How do I do that?
■ **Behaviours**	What am I doing?
■ **Environment**	What is going on?

A change at a higher level affects the levels below. The reverse, from the bottom to the top, is not always the case. You can learn to stick to the rules (behaviour), even if you think the rules are nonsense (belief). Good listening forms the basis for asking good questions. The way a person recites experiences is an indication for the (solution) level, where that person can (still) be found.

At the first three levels, it generally boils down to asking so-called solution-oriented questions. Learning about the environment, one's own behaviour and one's own capabilities is called "outside learning." A good meeting, coaching session or training course brings the solution closer. Learning at the belief, identity and spirituality levels is called

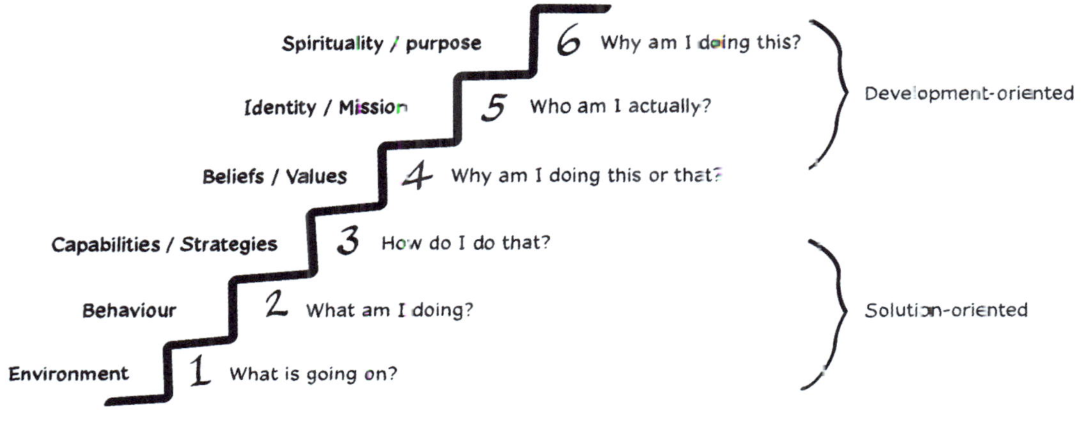

"inside learning" in this model. Questions that deal with these levels are called development-oriented questions. Peer supervision, coaching, supervision and sometimes psychotherapy are tools that can help take us to the next step. If the solutions no longer work at a certain level, it is necessary to jump to reach the next level. It is essential for a manager to discover at what level an employee experiences their problem and to give them the opportunity to take a step to the next level.

This is how the model works:

Level 1 Environment: What is going on?

If you define a problem at the environment level you can expect possible solutions at a level higher. The solution becomes apparent if the other person asks themself questions at the level of their own behaviour, encouraged by the questions you are asking.

You hear: "The frequent absenteeism in my department is starting to worry me. I am beginning to get really fed up. The result is that I can hardly achieve normal production levels". You bring up the other person's behaviour and ask: "What have you done to improve the situation? What else can you think of? What else might work? What probably will not work?"

Level 2 Behaviours: What am I doing?

If someone speaks of a problem in terms of their own behaviour, the solution then lies at the capability level.

You hear: "I have tried everything, but I haven't seen any improvement yet. How can I approach this colleague in a way that they will talk about the real reason they are missing work? My current approach has not worked. I will have to think of another way to approach this issue". You talk about the capabilities of the other person and ask: "How have you been handling that up until now? What were the effects? Is there something you would like to know about how to put an end to this problem? Do you know someone who could probably solve this type of issue easily? How would that person handle it?"

Level 3 Capabilities: How do I do it?

If a person expresses their problem in terms of their own capabilities, it is advisable to examine the level of the beliefs. Any questions you ask that touch upon that area can help you significantly.

You hear: I speak regularly with her whenever she is here, don't I? I think I give her enough support. That works well with others. Janine always promises to be better, but I don't see any difference yet. You bring up the (obstructive) beliefs and ask: How do you think your colleagues see you? What do they think about you if you discuss their absenteeism with them? What do you think of those opinions? Are they right or do they not see whom they are dealing with? How would you prefer them to see you?

The question: "What am I doing it all for?" still plays a leading and decisive role

Level 4 Beliefs: Why do I do this or that?
If the other person's story is full of beliefs about themself, others and the world around them, the question you should ask is how they see themself. Images that people have about themselves easily become self-fulfilling prophecies.

You hear: "I don't understand why this particular colleague doesn't seem to take me very seriously. She keeps telling me that she will do everything she can, but that doesn't last long. A couple of weeks later she starts calling in sick again." You bring up the identity level and ask: "How do you see yourself? What image (metaphor!) do you have of yourself? What expectations do you have of your work environment? What do you think is ideal in terms of relationships and working together with colleagues?"

Level 5 Identity: Who am I?
In this example, the manager refers to themself as a "reliable supporter" of their employees.

Adjusting and redefining this (self) image can help to look at the issue differently. You will help them even more by asking them questions that will make them think about the essence of leadership.

You hear: "I see myself in my leadership role chiefly as a reliable supporter. I support my people where I can, I stand up for them". You bring up meaningful issues and ask: "What do you think is the essence of good leadership? What is the most important point about the relationship between management and employee? Why is that important to you?"

Level 6 Spirituality: What am I doing it for?
The question for shaping your development: "Why am I doing it" plays a leading and decisive role in all human activity. Exploring the (possibly outdated) answers can help the other person to become aware of what their question (see level 1) refers to in the end(!). A change can be necessary to create a different effect in the environment.

Images that we have of ourselves easily become self-fulfilling prophecies

TASK

Think about an issue that has dragged on over time, which you would really like to change.

- Describe the desired situation. Finish with an essential question.
- Describe the current situation. Finish again with a good question.

Ask questions

- Describe the obstacles that stand in the way of moving from the current situation to the desired situation. Finish with a great question.
- Describe the sources (in yourself or in others) you can tap into to effect change. Finish with a question that would make even Einstein jealous.

... AND THE ART OF SURFING

At www.alberteinstein.nl you will find a number of links to websites with different inspirational stories about, and quotes by, Albert Einstein.

MAINSTREAM 3 STRUGGLING WITH THE ROLE

The art of sailing is that a sailor is faced with two different forces. She uses the elements and lets the wind, the seasons and the currents work for her. She also employs her own power to get the rudder and the sail into the best possible position. Her own power and the power of the elements are in line with one another in the best case scenario. Managers also employ their own personal power, experience, knowledge, skills and abilities. They also know the possibilities and impossibilities of the system and the context in which the manager takes on their role. Excellent managers know both forces, and make good use of them to keep their organisation on course.

KICK OFF

"As a manager I chiefly see myself as a goalkeeper." This was a quote by a company's department manager. This quote, in particular the metaphor, says a lot about how he sees his role. In his behaviour and his language (the outside) he "reveals" something about his thoughts (the inside) about his role. A role is foremost "an idea in the mind" according to developers of Group Relations Theory. What someone thinks about their role "in their head" directly affects what they do, for example, how they spend their time, what their priorities are. A central theme in this chapter is recent thoughts about the term "role." The question is how do you pick up or take on your role of manager effectively and efficiently.

QUESTIONS

- What metaphor would you use to describe your current role as a manager?
- Why did you choose this particular metaphor?
- What does the interpretation of your role mean to your daily activities?
- What is the power of your metaphor, applied to your role of manager?
- What could be a disadvantage?
- What do you definitely do and definitely not do as a manager, based on your chosen metaphor?
- Is there a different, more appealing metaphor that you would like to develop in your daily work?
- What difference would it make?
- What behavioural changes would be visible to your employees?

DIRECTION OF THOUGHT 1: AN IDEA IN YOUR MIND

Thinking about the what and the how of your role can help you better achieve your own goals and the goals of the organisation. A role is the externally visible manifestation of an internal system of knowledge, thoughts, emotions and, more importantly, will. The term "role" appears to be much more fruitful than the common terms "job" and "task." Job profiles and task descriptions are useful for legal protection purposes and for providing clarity about employment conditions, but they often create the impression that the work is clear, comprehensible and manageable. They suggest that it is crystal clear what your job is, thus you can get to work. A website for managers states: "Job descriptions provide clarity and ensure transparency of responsibilities and authority. That substantially prevents job conflicts." We know from experience that it is much more complicated than that. No-one can perform a task adequately by obediently adhering to that kind of description. What do we need? We need to set priorities, relate activities to new circumstances and make decisions under changing conditions. None of that can be specified accurately and completely beforehand.

The question to a number of middle managers, working in the same field, about how they saw their own roles produced a wide range of answers. They all worked with the same job and task descriptions, but the answers mirrored the different ways each of them perceived their role. One manager said: "I am a type of gateway for management," Another person said: "I see myself as a primus inter pares in my team. I am chiefly a sounding board for the team members in my department. "I am the oil in my department. Actually I am a jack-of-all-trades! The starter motor for my team! Initiator" or the "Goalkeeper." These managers, who are greatly dependent upon each other at work, were surprised and shocked by these significant differences. They thought that the job profile they were assigned, in combination with their task description, provided enough of a guideline to give direction to the way they perform their jobs. Now they realise that their behaviour was actually being guided by their perception of their role and that these differences were the source of many misunderstandings.

What someone is thinking "in their mind" about their role, as mentioned before, directly affects what they do, how they spend their time and what their priorities are. Except it is difficult when you cannot see what someone is thinking: a role is primarily an internal category. The idea of what the role entails lies somewhere in the connections between the hundred billion brain cells. The inside of each person consists of all kinds of emotions, meanings, perceptions, thoughts and intentions, and cannot be directly recognised by another person. Should you wish to know something about role perception, behaviour and language, you should watch out for logical clues.

The following statements, along with the related perceived behaviours, will give you an impression of how someone sees their role as a manager. The visible external side will give you a clue about the thoughts on the inside.

- "I spend a lot of time mediating in all types of issues."
- "I spend most of my time solving the hot issues on a day-to-day basis."
- "I put a lot of time into an abundance of monitoring activities."

An example of someone with a strong idea about her role was the director who always made one-sided decisions during meetings with her department managers, and always hit the table with the side of her hand. While observing this behaviour, you got a (first) impression of that 'idea in her mind." This director is obviously communicating implicit messages about how she sees the role of her department managers.

QUESTIONS

- What is your hypothesis of the idea this director has in her mind about her role?
- And what about the role of her department managers?

The solution for most issues with which you struggle as a manager cannot be found in the job profile or the task description

The solution for most of the issues you struggle with as a manager cannot be found in the job profile or task description. The invitation is to continue to reflect on everything that affects the way you fulfil your role. The following questions are food for thought:

- When is the organisation where you work successful?
- What employee behaviour will definitely contribute to this success?
- What behaviour is necessary on your part to cause that behaviour?

Someone who has taken on their role effectively will notice that the power factor ("It's a part of my job, it's in the job description!") plays an increasingly less significant part. Leaders who fulfil their role effectively will speak with authority and act from the authority they gain from adequately understanding their role. This is why people can be given power, but they can't be given authority!

DIRECTION OF THOUGHT 2: A ROLE IS NOT…

Taking on a role, in the above meaning, has nothing to do with playing a role in a play. You don't play a manager as if life and work are a play. You look at your daily work again and again to see what is necessary for you to take up your role. You struggle with the tension between the person you are and the person you believe the environment (the organisation and the context) is asking you to be. There is constant interaction inside your mind between the ideas you have about the person you are, the system in which you work and the role you play.

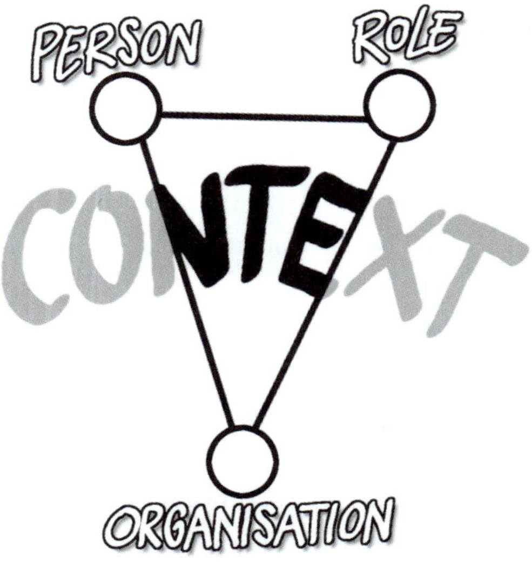

An example:

- **Personal level:** How do I view the role of chairperson and what are my own opportunities and boundaries?
- **Organisational level:** What do others in the organisation expect from me in my role as chairperson? What opportunities does this organisation give me to be successful in this role? How does the system facilitate my role?
- **Role level:** What is the main behavioural result of the considerations for me as chairperson? Taking up a role is serious business.

You take up a variety of different roles every day. Before you go to work you may take up the role of parent and partner in your family. While you are driving to work you fulfil the role of traffic participant. If you meet a friend during your journey to work, you take up the role of friend. When you start the day in a meeting, you enter into the role of chairperson. When you are in contact with your employees throughout the day, you are functioning in your role of manager. You fulfil as many roles as there are systems to which you belong.

The struggle with the role is endless. Even if you think that you are fulfilling your role as a parent well, you will notice now and then that you need to make adjustments. The father of a baby requires a different interpretation of the role than the father of a toddler, a teenager, or an adult son or daughter. And, the parenting ideas from the past century no longer fit with the opportunities and threats of today's society. The "family" system and its context are constantly being subjected to change. This makes demands on family roles: flexibility and creativity are a necessity! Every system and every organisation is also in a constant state of change. The context in which organisations look for their role is no less dynamic. The manager who does not take on the struggle will lose contact with the natural development process and will remove themself from the picture.

A man once saw a butterfly that was trying with all its might to free itself from its cocoon to enter into the world in a beautiful, new form. Feeling very sorry for the butterfly, the man took his pocket knife and carefully cut the cocoon open. He then took the little animal carefully into his hands and threw it up into the air. To his complete bewilderment, it fluttered helplessly down to the ground. By taking the work away from the butterfly to free itself from the cocoon, he had inadvertently robbed the little animal of the life-saving practice it needed to learn to fly.

A healthy intrinsic encouragement and real interest form the foundation for taking up the role. Then, it is also a matter of knowledge: having the capacity to apply a wide range of skills that a manager should possess. Finally, it is a matter of endless practice and adjustments. Nothing was more difficult than learning how to walk, but who is still surprised that they can walk now? Practice, practice and more practice by falling down and getting up again!

These three basic conditions – the foundation, the capacity, the practice – for successful leadership can be summarised by a compact slogan: “Will, skill & drill”.

Have you ever had the privilege to become a mother or father? You must have been bombarded by all kinds of well-meaning advice from the people around you? It quickly became apparent that all those fine stories had little to do with reality, to which you looked to guide you in the way you wanted to be a mother or father of your child. A role cannot be taught, but it can be learnt. It’s not about the recipe, but about the meal that will be served. The quality of the meal goes beyond the method of preparation: presentation of the food is important, the wonderful aromas are also essential, as well as where the food is served. And what about the guests with whom you are sharing the meal?

There is a teacher and a student for everyone in every organisation

If the people around you embrace their own roles well, you will have a better chance of being able to learn a lot about your own role. The following applies to your employees: the better you embrace your role as manager, the more likely they will be successful at defining and embracing their own roles. In a good organisation everyone, from management to workers on the floor, can learn from each other. In every organization there is a teacher and a student for everyone. Experience shows that the way in which the highest people in the hierarchy embrace their role will affect the behaviour on the work floor. What behaviour in your organisation you want to stimulate is an important question for every manager. A manager who only communicates about money will create calculating employees on the work floor. The more a director knows how to promote independent thinking, the bigger the chance that the employees will assume their own responsibility.

QUESTIONS

From whom did you learn important things about your current management role? Who inspired you? What was the main thing that inspired you? How does the way you take on your role now provide meaning? And, what behaviour do you want to cause?

DIRECTION OF THOUGHT 3: EXPLORING THE SYSTEM

Three related processes affect how you take up the role.

Process 1 Find

It is absolutely necessary to know the objective of the system where you have a role. As long as you don't know what objective the system has, you will continue to search for your role without much chance of success. The knowledge that there is an organisation and customers or service users, and whether you are in the role of service provider, maintainer, administrator, developer ... offers a strong basis when searching for the role. The question is primarily, how a person's own efforts contribute to the interest of the users. It also helps to look at the organisation from the eyes of those users.

By adequately taking up a role, you learn to relate your own capabilities and responsibilities to the context of the system.

> You can only take up a role successfully if you know what the system is for

Process 2 Make

The search for the role ends with finding it. You initially have a picture of it (in your mind). You will then create that role, fulfil it and expand it. The best way is to continuously ask questions about how the system works in which you are fulfilling a role. It all boils down to building the behaviour that fits with the role for which you are searching. Questions you can ask include:

- "What are the typical cultural aspects of this system"?
- "Are there typical (explicit or implicit) expectations that are communicated by others within this system"?
- "What do I have to do to be successful within this system"?
- "Must I take up my role as manager in the same way for all employees? How can I differentiate the role"?

A role cannot be specified beforehand, unlike jobs and tasks. Again, it's not about the recipe, but about the meal; it's about experiencing the meal! Whoever is consciously searching, finding and fulfilling a role is primarily focusing on issues within his own range of knowledge, abilities and skills (the psychological role) and issues within the system (the sociological role). Your own personality and power within the system facilitate and limit you in taking up your role.

Process 3 Take up

Once you have searched, found and created your role, the next step is to fulfil it effectively. If you take up your role in this way, you will be doing the system, and everyone in it, a big favour. You will become a co-owner of the objective of the organisation. You never finish taking up a role. You will always struggle with the role, because the contexts of the different systems in which you play your roles are constantly changing. Someone who takes up the role of a teacher now in the same way as a teacher did thirty years ago is not doing his students any favours, let alone the school or society. A text like "I have been doing it this way for thirty years!" shows that the changing system had no influence on the way that person was taking up his role. Someone in this position will automatically be "sidelined." Taking up a role is constantly subject to changed views and self-assessments, and changing context. At the same time, growth is necessary of your self-awareness, your own abilities, emotions, thoughts and values, as well as the skill to evaluate the context, to see the opportunities, the threats, the differences and the similarities. The manager who wants to avoid the healthy and necessary struggle and holds firm to job profiles and task descriptions, misjudges the dynamics of their daily job. The struggle with your role is a flexible and dynamic act.

DIRECTION OF THOUGHT 4: MIRRORS AND WINDOWS

Once you have taken up a role, it will become easier to find the essentials of that role. Once you have found the role, you will notice that the role becomes easier to create. Once you have created your own role, it will cost you less effort to fulfil your role. If you keep searching and asking questions about your role, you will end up in an upwards spiral towards better knowledge, skills and ability. What's more, the better the people around you are able to take up their role, the better the chance they will learn from it. Employees who come to you with the right questions about the right things, make it a lot easier for you to find, make and take up your own role.

In order to effectively take up your role, it is worth taking a hard and critical look at yourself in the mirror from time to time. You will see something that you can be proud of and that can make you happy! But sometimes you will see something that you have questions about or that you worry about. Knowing yourself is necessary to better understand what makes you successful and sometimes what makes you so ineffective. However you look at it, your own behaviour is the key to each desired change.

QUESTION

What is the most important question if you look at your own behaviour as a manager in the mirror?

A good start is to look in the mirror and increase your self-knowledge. But it is not enough to just look in the mirror. To see a new perspective, it is also necessary to open new windows. Each window offers a different perspective on reality. Each perspective adds something to the mental pictures you already had. Together, they form the mental image you have of the system in which you work. The question is not what reality is, but how you look at reality. This determines what you see!

QUESTION

What are the first questions that come to mind if you look at the system (your organisation, your department or your team) more closely?

... AND THE ART OF SURFING

At www.alberteinstein.nl you will find an article that discusses the question of how students at a school struggle with their role on a daily basis: Taking up the pupil role!

MIRRORS

REFLECTIONS ON THE PERSON YOU ARE

MIRROR 1: IT'S ALL ABOUT YOUR POINT OF VIEW

An old king, who had no children, thought deeply about who he would appoint to be his successor. He spoke to his people during the evening news: I will pass on the crown to the person who can bring me something that is one of a kind, someone who can protect the country, someone who can take care of the land, who can make decisions, who can listen to advice given by others and who can have fun. The person who can do all that will be expected at the court." The king was dying to see if princes or princesses would present themselves. Perhaps finally everyone would notice how difficult it is to be king!

The next day, the palace garden was full of people. There were even long queues of people up to the palace. Did all these people come to apply as a prince or princess? It was too much for the king to bear. He summoned the court's psychologist. "Well, Sire", said the psychologist, "Each person has brought something that is one of a kind: those people have brought themselves! Everyone has the ability to do the other things you asked. And anyone who cannot do something, can learn how."

The king cried out in surprise: "That means that anyone can become a prince or a princess, and whoever isn't one yet, can learn how to become one!" He had never looked at it in that way before. That same evening, the news was broadcast that the king would crown all his subjects prince or princess and that he had also decided that he wasn't going to die for a very long time.

QUESTION

The first mirror you look into, strangely enough, will show you a window: the window through which you can see yourself, the people around you and your environment. It is simply a matter of how you look at it, particularly, how YOU look at it!

This mirror shows you how you look at the world around you (through coloured glasses), how your opinions about yourself, about others and about the world you live in influence your observations.

What is the ideal pair of glasses that will give you a healthy view of yourself and a healthy insight into a workable relationship with the people around you?

TASK

Reflect on a recent conversation you had with one of your employees, a conversation that made an impression on you. Try and remember it as clearly as possible. What was discussed? How was it discussed? What struck you about the way your employee held themself, looked, spoke and listened?

Specify:

- What you think this employee's opinion is of themself.
- What this employee thinks your opinion is of them.
- What you think your employee's opinion is of you.
- What you think this employee's opinion is of others (colleagues).

And also:

- How you view this employee.
- How this employee views you.
- How you view other employees.

DIRECTION OF THOUGHT 1: I'M OK, YOU'RE OK

If you listen and look carefully, you will hear and see how one of your employees sees themself, how they look at you and how they perceive and assess other people in the organisation. It can differ substantially. They can communicate "I am quite smart" or "I am firm and strong." But they might see themself as inferior, helpless, second class or powerless. During a conversation, they might perceive others in their immediate surroundings, including you, as people who can't be trusted, people who are good for nothing. On the other hand, these employees might see others mainly as a source of esteem and as partners who work well together as a team.

How you perceive yourself colours the glasses you use to perceive others.

Now we will ask you, as a manager, how do you see yourself? As someone who breaks ground to get things done, or as a co-operative supervisor? A director once said: "I have only been parachuted into the role of director!" This said more about self-perception (passive, helpless, at the mercy of the whims of the organisation and a culture full of "bombs and grenades") than about his surroundings. Do you really think you are somebody, or do you not value yourself very highly? How you perceive yourself has an effect on how others see you. Your intentions, the decisions you make about yourself, about others and about the organisation are based on your self-perception.

What position you take in life and in your career makes quite a difference. Summarised in a metaphor: it makes quite a difference what window someone is looking through to see the world around them. The following categories illustrate the extremes:

"I'M OK, YOU'RE OK" → I+, YOU+
"I'M OK, YOU'RE NOT OK" → I+, YOU−
"I'M NOT OK, YOU'RE OK" → I−, YOU+
"I'M NOT OK, YOU'RE NOT OK" → I−, YOU−

Thomas Harris (1969) wrote a book about it entitled I'm OK, You're OK. It became a worldwide bestseller! It looks like this in a quadrant:

With a little imagination you can see four windows here. Four windows on the world. If you dare to look in the mirror, you can see which of the four windows reflects your basic outlook on life. By observing your own behaviour and paying attention to the feedback you receive, you will be able to better understand why you "choose" a certain window at a certain time.

"I never receive any feedback," said the teacher who had seen classes full of students, hunched over in their seats, groaning and moaning, cheating, messing about and being bored for twenty years.

Although one of the windows is your basic life window, you also look through one of the other windows from time to time. This gives you more insight into your own behaviour in different situations. The basic life window is based on your earlier life experiences, all types of internalised messages that are referred to as 'Parent' in Mirror 2. Because your outlook on life is often anchored in the deep waters of your childhood (this is called 'Child' in Mirror 2), it is not so easy to give up this outlook. But, by better understanding the underlying motives, you will be more successful in assessing what merit the messages from the old days have today. In Mirror 2, this is called (the function of) 'Adult.' This will assist in discovering how you can think and live authentically and autonomously.

TASK

Are you wondering what your favourite window is?

Ask two or three colleagues to circle the statement in each block that suits you best. Ask them to be truthful. There is nothing better than honest feedback! It will help you most. Circle the number next to the statement in each group that best describes you.

Be honest with yourself – don't just pick whatever you think is the 'best' answer.

A	1	I tend to interrupt others when they are speaking
	2	I prefer to take a back seat in groups and let others take the lead
	3	I do my best to avoid situations where you're expected to give an opinion
	4	I let other people finish what they are saying before I speak
B	1	I usually think that other people know best
	2	I stand up for myself when I feel that I'm right and expect others to do the same
	3	I insist that I'm right and expect others to go along with me
	4	I don't see any point in pushing my ideas as people rarely appreciate them
C	1	I resist making decisions or taking advice from others
	2	I let other people make decisions for me
	3	I make my own decisions based on what I feel is right and appropriate
	4	I often make decisions for other people
D	1	I tend to keep my voice low and avoid eye contact to prevent attention being drawn to me
	2	I sometimes speak loudly and expect to make quite an impact
	3	I can't be bothered to communicate much
	4	I generally match my level of communication to suit the circumstances
E	1	I tend to blame and find fault with others
	2	I sometimes hide my feelings and just go along with others
	3	I do my best to understand the feelings of others before letting them know how I feel
	4	I don't often feel that strongly about anything

F	1	I let others get what they want but I often feel resentful about it
	2	I talk through problems before they occur and find ways of coping with them when they do
	3	I make sure that things turn out the way I want them to
	4	I really don't mind if other people get their own way
G	1	I hold back on decisions so that others will make them for me
	2	I tend to avoid facing problems and keep putting decisions off until tomorrow
	3	I deal with my own problems and make my own decisions
	4	I provide solutions for people who seem unable to decide for themselves
H	1	I consider myself capable and equal to others
	2	I consider myself weaker and less capable than others
	3	I consider myself stronger and more capable than others
	4	I consider that most people are weak, including me
I	1	I avoid taking responsibility as it only gets you blamed when things don't work out
	2	I accept my responsibilities and am clear about what others are responsible for
	3	I take on responsibility for as much as possible, including the work of others
	4	I prefer it when someone else takes responsibility and I can follow their lead

Windows on the World - Scoring

Step 1. Transfer your scores to the summary below, against the question numbers, and add up each column.

Q.A	4	A	2	B	1	C	3	D
Q.B	2	A	1	B	3	C	4	
Q.C	3	A	2	B	4	C	1	
Q.D	4	A	1	B	2	C	3	D
Q.E	3	A	2	B	1	C	4	D
Q.F	2	A	4	B	3	C	1	D
Q.G	3	A	1	B	4	C	2	D
Q.H	1	A	2	B	3	C	4	D
Q.I	2	A	4	B	3	C	1	D

Total A	*Total B*	*Total C*	*Total D*

Step 2. Now draw a bar chart of your scores by making horizontal lines at the score points.

Total score

8

7

6

5

4

3

2

1

0	A - win-win assertive	B – lose-win accommodating	C – win-lose aggressive	D – lose-lose apathetic

DIRECTION OF THOUGHT 2: NOT A HAPPY PICTURE?

The manager (or the employee) who mainly views the world through window I- YOU- has a different job/path than his colleague who views the world through window I+ You+. Try taking a look through the windows with a negative scenario:

+ – Your life doesn't count too much!

The manager who looks through this window will generally blame others for problems at work. That often makes employees feel that they are being 'belittled' or kept on a line. This attitude often makes them feel like they are literally "be-littled." This attitude creates distance: people are afraid to get close; they hide information from the manager. Managers who show this behaviour are often isolated from others.

While it is crucial to get the attention they so deeply need, this manager not only focuses their feedback on the issue at hand, but also often focuses on the person. Verbally: "You can't do it like that. This report can't go to the council like that." Non-verbal, underlying message: "I didn't expect much better from you anyway." Their style is dominating, controlling, demanding, sometimes angry, often blind to nuance and complexity, full of monocausal thinking in cause and effect. Their underlying motto appears to be Attack is the best form of defence.

– + My life doesn't have much value!

The person looking through this window often feels powerless and helpless. The manager with this basic outlook on life is usually friendly, a good listener, not very demanding, easy-going, very touchy/feely ("That's terrible, isn't it?") and very empathetic ("Wow, that was very clever of you!"). This leader is looking for a comfortable situation for themself, where they can avoid problems and conflicts because exercising power is not an option. This leader often has a (sometimes physical) inconvenience that stops them from delivering what is expected of them. “I had such a headache again that I just couldn’t get to that report.” Or: “I become depressed when the leaves start falling.” Feedback often hides behind a question: “It’s probably a stupid question but what is the best way to set up that report?”

This leader won’t cause a lot of trouble, but you also cannot expect much enjoyment, let alone results, from this person.

– – Life has no value!

The person looking through this window is losing their interest in life and in work. This loss will lead to cynicism in the end: difficult for others, but deadly for themself. The cynic doesn’t see themself or others in a positive light. They are close to despair. They give little feedback and the feedback they do give is often unintentional. It is characterised by a deep sigh. You rarely see this attitude in people in a leading position! This attitude usually manifests itself in an earlier stage. If not, everyone yearns for the day that this person finally leaves the organisation, usually not of their own accord!

DIRECTION OF THOUGHT 3: THE HEALTHY WINDOW

Harris’s book sells through edition after edition. Evidently, its title and content touch upon something real. It’s not about being OK with everything someone does. It is more fundamental than that. The question is whether you are ready to accept and value yourself and other persons unconditionally. In a book about TA for children, the author explains that “being OK with something” can best be understood by looking at what you are worth to your parents or to the people who raised you. Ask them how much money they would ask if they were to sell you. Even though they would like to string you up sometimes, they wouldn’t want to miss you for all the money in the world. You are important because you are here! Children, and even adults, usually feel in their bones whether or not that is the case.

+ + Life is worth living!

This is the healthy life window. The manager who has made this their life window will handle questions, issues and problems constructively. This manager is free from a not OK feeling about themself. This gives them space for OK + in relationship to others. In the case of a ++ attitude, there is no (more) adjusting to earlier (childhood) experiences. Their way of thinking is genuine, autonomous and based on facts from the here-and-now. The attitude is constructive, rational, co-operative, reflective and productive. This manager strives towards consensus, considers alternatives, wants to have all the questions, issues and problems on and above the table.

Feedback mainly focuses on the issue and not on the person

This manager is focused on personal growth and on the growth of the employees. Feedback is mainly given about issues, not about the person. These leaders have healthy decision-making processes in healthy organisations.

TASK

Review the following pieces of dialogue. Which windows on the world do you believe are wide open to you?

A: That report is still not as it should be.
B: I know I never do these things right the first time.

A: How are you after that altercation with the secretary?
B: I think I can get along well with them.

A: I suggest you first ask the people in your department.
B: You know they can't keep an eye on all those things anyway.

A: What are you going to do in the short-term to improve the morale of your team?
B: Don't ask me. I am tired of that bunch!

A: Well done people, this is how we're going to proceed! I assume you don't have any questions!
B: Okay boss!

An ineffective outlook on life can develop into a ++ outlook on life by ++ experiences with the people around you: colleagues, managers and others in your surrounding area. Communicating with authentic, reflective and co-operative people will give you the chance to grow and see yourself as OK. Then your ability to see others as OK will also grow over time. This doesn't mean that you always approve of the other person's behaviour. It just means that you can see the other person as someone, just like you, who can think independently, someone who can be reflective and creative, and someone who is worth loving.

MIRROR 2: INTENTIONS VERSUS EFFECTS

"And what are you drinking, John? Beer, or perhaps a whisky? There is Scotch, Canadian, Irish and a touch of blended."

"No thanks Chris, I'll have a glass of water."

"Water, I have Evian, still, fizzy, flavoured…"

"No, just a glass of water, tap water,

"How about some ice?"

"Really no, just hold a glass under the tap."

"I'll put a Sicilian olive in it for you."

'No Chris, I really don't want an olive."

"Oh, wait, you want something medicinal with it. What kind do you want,, Alka Seltzer, Andrew's, Nurofen, or Aspro…?"

"Man, there's nothing wrong with me! OK then, go ahead and give me a vodka and tomato juice…"

"No, you will have a big glass of water, John, and then you will lie down. Boys, let John go. John is not feeling well!"

QUESTIONS

This mirror confronts you with one of the most important tools of a leader: communication. You can use this mirror to discover your own communications style. You will also see how your communication style affects others. Usually successful, sometimes not. What makes your style so successful? What can you do or not do to improve the effects of your communication? From a professional point of view, what are the options that work better than "that's just how I am?"

TASKS

1. Reflect on a dialogue you were recently involved in. A conversation that left you dissatisfied for example. How did the conversation begin? What did you say? How did the other person react? How did your conversation progress? You can also write it down word for word.
2. Now that it's clear what was said, it is worthwhile asking yourself what was communicated between the lines (!). Create a film script about it and think what can be added in the text and in the margins about other non-verbal characteristics of the dialogues: posture, tone, volume of voices, tempo of speech, facial expressions, gestures?
3. What determined the success or failure of the dialogue for you? What were the factors related to the content of the dialogue? What were the factors in the non-verbal area?
4. What are your conclusions? And above all: what new questions do you have now?

DIRECTION OF THOUGHT 1: EGO-STATES

There is a funny joke about communication. A woman says to her husband: "I sometimes feel like we are talking to each other without really making contact." Her husband responded: "Yes, we are dear. That's called communication." Surprised she said: "Oh really? And, what's it called when we talk to each other and actually make contact?" He said: "Quarrelling dear!" Talking to each other without making contact is a frequent form of communication. And so is quarrelling for that matter. The art is to keep communication going if you so desire and to break it off if that seems better. Always with the idea to be as effective as possible. The meaning of your communication depends on the effect you create!

The meaning of your communication depends on the effect you create

The reasons for success and failure in communications surrounding work can be understood from patterns that play a role in communication. Transactional Analysis (TA) provides clear insight. The founder of this practical theory is Eric Berne (1910-1971), an American psychiatrist from the psychoanalytical area. See his book *The Structure and Dynamics of Organisations and Groups* (1975). A key concept from TA is the ego-state concept. An ego-state is a "way of being" that can be observed in each individual's behaviour (=communication). Each ego-state has a positive and negative side.

Each person's personality consists of three parts, or three "ways of being." Berne drew these three ego-states as three circles on top of each other.

CHILD Ego-state

Whenever you think, feel and behave in the same way as when you were a child, you are in Child. You still do a lot of things you used to do as a child. Spontaneously breaking out into laughter (or crying), having fun, being curious, enjoying life, pouting or moaning. For example, you are enthusiastic: 'It's crazy, isn't it..." or hurt: "Ouch, you're hurting me...", proudly: "Look at me...", sulking: 'No, I don't want to...", or frustrated: "Did I waste all my time and energy on..." The Child in you is holding onto thoughts, feelings and behaviours that you developed while you were growing up. The Adapted Child focuses on parental boundaries and expectations. The Child can literally adjust (+) or rebel (-). The Natural Child is spontaneous and creative (+) or does what you want to do without thinking about anyone else (-).

ADULT Ego-state

Whenever you gather information, consider possibilities or make real decisions, you are thinking in your Adult state. This is the part of the personality that is characterised by the here-and-now thoughts, feelings and behaviours. Whenever you are in your Adult ego-state, you describe the things you have observed without judging their value and without directly recalling and expressing feelings. For example, when providing information: "I read that...", "Look, that's how.... works", or stating something: "There is no proof that....", or asking for information: "Have you ever tried that?" The Adult in you is logical and solves problems. Everything that is a here-and-now answer to things going on around you emanates from your Adult ego-state.

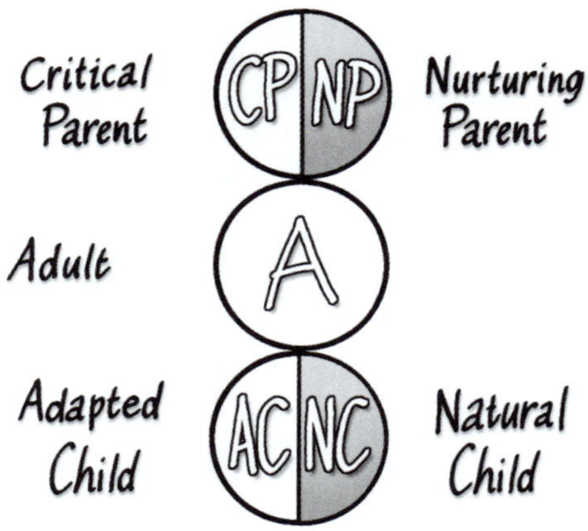

PARENT Ego-state

Whenever you think, feel and act like your parents, educators or other important people in your life, you are in your Parent Ego-state. You say similar things to others as your parents or educators used to say to you. You use comparable values and standards that were used by the other important people in your life. It is like you are talking with the voice of your "parents." It is internalising the behaviour of people who took care of you at a time when you were most impressionable. For example, critical: "Shouldn't you...", compelling: ".... because I said so!", corrective: "Don't do .....like that", or caring: "I think it would be good for you if you....". The Critical Parent in you draws limits and offers structure (+), or is too critical and dominating (-). The Nurturing Parent is caring and gives compliments and attention (+) or is too concerned and indulgent (-).

The Woollams and Brown (1978) table below provides insight into better recognising and understanding the behaviours and activities of the different Ego-states in daily communication.

	CRITICAL PARENT	NURTURING PARENT	ADULT	NATURAL CHILD	ADAPTED CHILD
WORDS	bad	good	correct	wow !	can't
	should	nice	how	fun	wish
	ought	I love you	what	want	try
	must	cute	why	won't	hope
	always	splendid	practical	ouch	please
	ridiculous	tender	quantity	hi!	thank you
VOICE	critical	loving	even	free	whiny
	condescending	comforting	precise	loud	defiant
	disgusted	concerned	monotone	energetic	placating
	firm	sugary		happy	demanding
GESTURES	pointing finger	open arms	thoughtful	uninhibited	pouting
or	frowning	accepting	alert	loose	sad
EXPRESSION	angry	smiling	open	spontaneous	innocent
POSTURE	shoulders up	leaning forward	erect	loose	collapsed
	hands on hips	head in front of body		relaxed	closed tight
				agile	
ATTITUDE	judgmental	understanding	interested	curious	demanding
	moralistic	caring	observant	fun-loving	compliant
	authoritarian	giving	evaluative	changeable	ashamed

DIRECTION OF THOUGHT 2: EGOGRAM

Task

Use the following questionnaire to make an egogram. You can show which ego-states set the tone for your communication style and which ones you are less likely to use. Note the score next to each statement based on how well each one applies to your behaviour. Then record the scores on the score sheet and draw a bar chart.

INSTRUCTIONS

For each statement, allocate a score to show how much the behaviour is like the way you behave:

not true for me 0 partly true for me 1 moderately true for me 2 extremely true for me 3

ITEM	SCORE	
1.		I tell people firmly how they should behave.
2.		I tend to reason things out before acting.
3.		I do as I'm told.
4.		I behave sympathetically towards people with problems.
5.		I really enjoy being with other people.
6.		I enjoy taking care of people.
7.		I enjoy solving problems in a systematic and logical way.
8.		I tell people what to do.
9.		I let people know how I really feel without embarrassment.
10.		I am polite and courteous.
11.		I do the opposite to what people expect.
12.		When someone is new, I make an effort to show them where everything is.
13.		I can stay calm in a crisis.
14.		When I know I'm right, I insist that others listen to me.
15.		I ask a lot of questions when I'm curious.
16.		I am very enthusiastic about my work.
17.		People seem to expect me to know the answer.
18.		I'm asked to take care of new members of staff.
19.		I get on well with people who are polite to me.
20.		I keep on thinking logically even under pressure.
21.		My working style is systematic and logical.
22.		I dress to match the sort of outfits that other people wear to work.
23.		I do things for people when I think they can't manage for themselves.
24.		I can quote my previous experience when problems occur.
25.		People tell me I'm creative and inventive.
26.		I prefer to take control rather than following someone else's lead.
27.		I fuss over people too much.
28.		I'm over-emotional compared to others.
29.		I expect my manager to set my terms of reference.
30.		I take all points of view into account when making decisions.
31.		I encourage people to test out their own capabilities.
32.		People complain that I'm bossy.
33.		I spend time enjoying myself.
34.		People tell me I'm especially courteous.
35.		I'm noted for my even temper and balanced comments.
36.		I show my feelings whether I am happy or sad, so that people can congratulate or sympathise with me.

37.	I've looked after someone even though they could have managed on their own.
38.	I'm tempted to analyse jokes, which spoils them for others.
39.	People do as I tell them.
40.	I go along too readily with what other people want.

Personal Styles Questionnaire - Scoring

Step 1. Transfer your scores to the summary below, against the question numbers, and add up each column.

	SCORE		SCORE		SCORE		SCORE		SCORE
1		4		2		3		5	
8		6		7		10		9	
14		12		13		11		15	
17		18		20		19		16	
24		23		21		22		25	
26		27		30		29		28	
32		31		35		34		33	
39		37		38		40		36	
Total									
	Controlling Parent		Nurturing Parent		Adult		Adapted Child		Natural Child

Now turn to the next page for Step 2.

Step 2. Now draw a bar chart of your responses by marking horizontal lines at the score points.

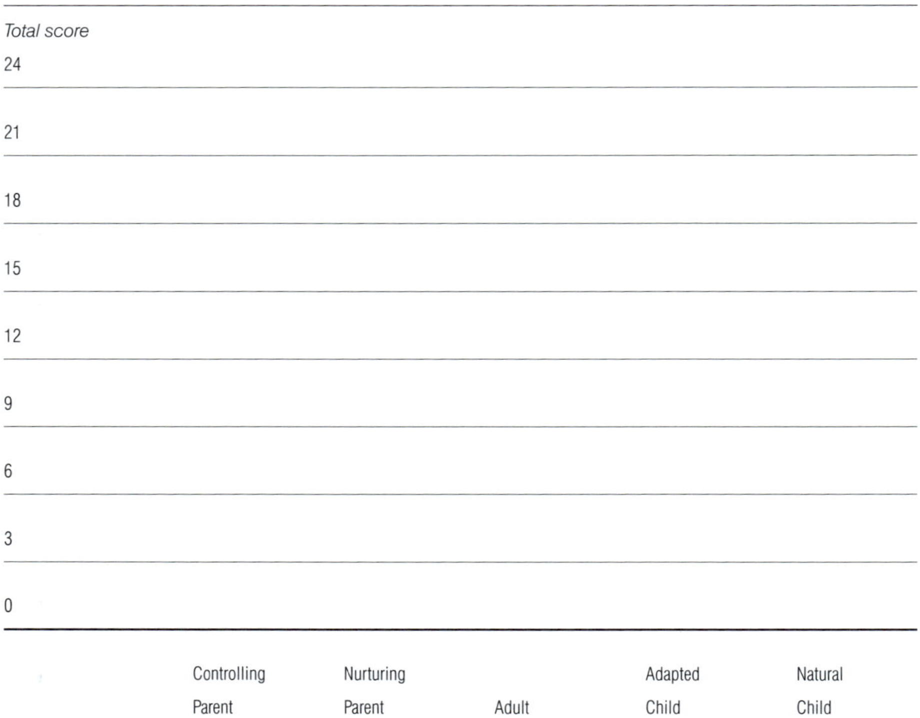

DIRECTION OF THOUGHT 3: TRANSACTIONS

It takes at least two of you to communicate on the work floor. You can use the TA model to understand who is talking to whom. You can observe a "conversation" in your mind between your Parent and your Child. "Do you really want to do that? Be careful!" Child: "I really want to. It can be safe!" Use your Adult ego-state to gather all the necessary information before you make a decision. If you look at the communication through the TA model, there is always an exchange (a stimulus and a response) between your ego-states and the ego-states of another person or persons. The stimulus from one and the response by the other together form a transaction. Berne points out three communication rules.

Rule 1

Communication can continue indefinitely as long as the transactions remain complementary.

Transactions are complementary if someone addresses another person's particular ego-state and the other person responds using that ego-state. An employee asks you: "When can we talk about my questions regarding the task?" He is using his Adult ego-state to address your Adult ego-state. You "choose" to respond from your Adult ego-state: "I don't have an exact time. My secretary has my calendar information." Both of you can then see how to set up the meeting in both of your calendars. During a progress meeting with one of your employees you say in a harsh voice: "You really need to deliver the agreed documents within a few days!" The tone and word choice are typical of the Critical Parent. The Adapted Child in your employee nods.

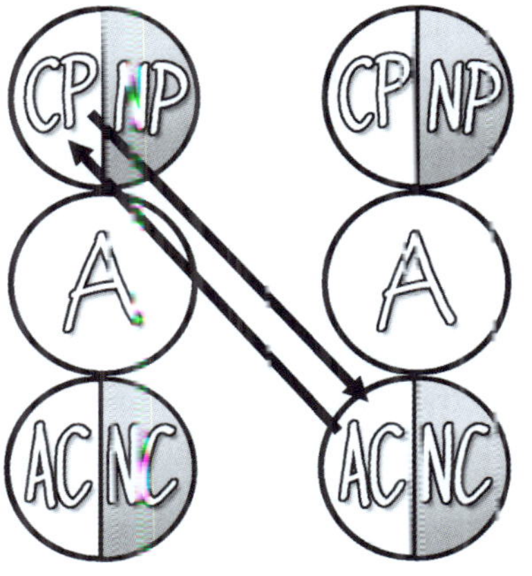

Two colleagues talk to each other using their Critical Parent, criticising the way their organisation is managed: "They have no idea what takes place on the work floor. They need to pay more attention to the real issues!" A workgroup is working together to prepare a presentation. They laugh a little and then they concentrate on the task at hand. You can tell by looking at their faces that the transactions usually emanate from their Natural Child.

Rule 2

A break in communication occurs whenever a transaction is crossed.

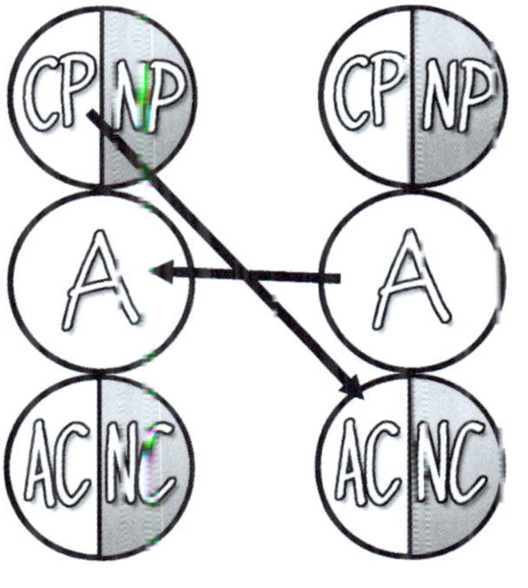

Complementary transactions often provide a lot of satisfaction and can continue for a long time, until one of the two responds differently, resulting in a crossed transaction. If transactions are crossed, the communication will occur differently. The exchanges will be shorter and will not be as smooth. The employee who used his Adult to make an appointment about a task he didn't quite understand receives the response: "This is the third time you are stuck on this task!" The content, the tone and even the expression make it clear that this is a Critical Parent talking. There is a big chance that the employee's Adapted Child mode thinks: "Ouch! Watch out," and then continues in a light, apologetic voice: "Sorry, but I really don't know what to do!"

Crossed transactions interrupt the conversation or take it to a different subject. Therefore, you can use the crossed transaction to your advantage to manage the conversation. Someone excitedly and enthusiastically tells a colleague about an upcoming promotion that comes with a big salary increase. They are as happy as a child (Natural Child) and want to "celebrate together". However, the colleague responds from her Critical Parent. "I think you're making too much of a fuss about it." The only way to not interrupt the communication is to change the ego-state. After a brief moment of confusion, the other person uses Adult to calmly say: "This is the first time I can go to the next step in my career."

iA crossed message also occurs in the middle of a conversation if people are complaining and moaning about "the quality of employees today". Someone suggests: "Let's go over the points once again!" The others ignore the suggestion so that the complaints can continue (Adapted Child), or they go along with the suggestion and leave their Adapted Child and enter into their Adult to review the issue more closely. It is sometimes handy to cross a transaction, for example, at a time when an employee uses Adapted Child for the umpteenth time to appeal to your Nurturing Parent. "I don't know what to do any more. I don't feel at ease with that team at all." (AC). That type of question can be countered with the simple question: "What do you think should happen?" or "What have you done so far to ensure that it will operate better?"

(A). At that moment you consciously use a crossed transaction. You force or help the other person to reflect and to take action themself by responding to this Child action through your Adult ego-state instead of your Parent ego-state (thus, not taking care of them).

Rule 3

The result of a hidden transaction is determined by the psychological (non-verbal) level and not by the social (verbal) level. Hidden transactions are both pleasant and difficult. Something different occurs with these transactions at the social, verbal level than at the psychological, usually non-verbal level.

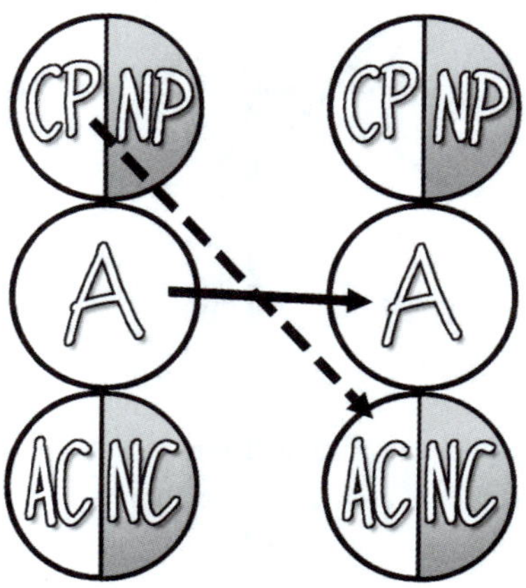

The meeting has just started and the chairperson asks: "Have you read through all the documents, Fred?" It sounds like the chairman is asking for information, but if you look and listen carefully, you hear the Critical Parent in the chairperson's question. Without saying a word he says: "You are probably just as ill-prepared as you were the last time!" Fred responds to the look in the chairperson's eyes and to the tone of his voice. Using his Adapted Child, Fred says: "Geez, what's that all about? I will contribute my fair share today you know!" The chairperson's response: "That is not what I meant; I was just curious whether you have had the time to prepare properly", is only half true at best. You can imagine that the hidden transaction can lead to a lot of communicative misunderstandings and noise. The misunderstandings can be conscious or subconscious. It is essential to bring subconscious misunderstandings out in the open because they could result in unnecessary disputes.

Hidden transactions are often used for psychological games and to manipulate others (see further under Window 2). This occurs because the psychological, non-verbal level message prevails in communication. As long as this corresponds with what is being communicated at the social level, there is no problem. In any case: the non-verbal message (positive or negative hidden message) determines how well the communication will progress.

Hidden transactions are not always "unfair":
It is sometimes the speaker's intention to create the double meaning: for example, the case of two colleagues who clearly like each other a lot and are always looking for each other's company. They regularly conduct an "interesting" (Adult) conversation about how things are going in the department. Their facial expressions and their voices (Natural Child) divulge that they want to see each other as more than just colleagues. A good observer can easily notice that.

TASK

In a TV programme, an elderly gentleman said once to the interviewer: "If I sigh, my wife pours me some coffee!" The interviewer responded quick-wittedly to this remark with a follow-up question: "And what do you get if you sigh twice? Cappuccino?!" Based on what you have learnt about these transactions, what can you say about the above "communication" between the man and his wife, and between the man and the interviewer?

... AND THE ART OF SURFING

There is another questionnaire on the website at www.einstein.nl where you can create an egogram of your organisation. Are you curious about which Ego-states dominate your organisation? Log onto the website, go to Mirror 2, answer the questions and you will see the results right away!

MIRROR 3: WHEN "CAN" TURNS INTO "MUST"!

Even now having a pleasant lunch with your colleagues, the difference in (working) style is noticeable. Colleague Quick hardly takes any time for her lunch. She appears to prefer eating lunch on the run. Right when she wants to leave ("There are other things to do"), colleague Meticulous arrives. His lunch looks perfect: the meal has been prepared with great care and meets all the requirements of the food pyramid. Enthusiastic as always, colleague Action comes around the corner. Before he reaches the table, where his colleagues are eating their lunch, he has already talked to different interesting people and has come across a few new ideas, which he would like to work with right after lunch. Colleague Pamper has already noticed that he will not get around to actually eating his lunch. She makes sure that he gets a sandwich and she pours coffee for everyone and cleans up everything that has been left on the table. Nothing is too much for her to make others happy. She's a real treasure! And, where is colleague Firm? He doesn't care about lunch and he can skip it: It's a waste of time; he always has a banana if he gets really hungry. When he comes in for a cup of strong coffee, Pamper is there to pour his coffee: "A little cream, Firm? Colleague Firm is nowhere to be seen. Meticulous has just unfolded his napkin and is carefully peeling a hard-boiled egg. Nobody knows where Action is. He's probably wherever the "news" is. A strange group of colleagues. However, together they can accomplish a lot. But sometimes it's a disaster…

QUESTIONS

You will be able to recognise your own working style by looking in this mirror. This recognition raises questions. Is there a certain pattern in how I approach my work? What is characteristic of me? How does my working style often benefit me or give me pleasure? How does my working style limit me sometimes? Can I learn to use my strengths better and to better manage my weaknesses? What about the working styles of the people around me?

TASK

1. Have you noticed that you have a preferred working style? Can you explain this style more in detail? What are the strengths of this pattern? Can you also specify the weaknesses of this characteristic working style?
2. Can you provide a couple of characteristics of someone at work who is somewhat difficult to work with? What are their strengths? What are the weaknesses in their approach? What difficulty do you experience in their approach?

DIRECTION OF THOUGHT 1: TOO MUCH OF A GOOD THING

The well-known model by Daniel Ofman (2001) teaches us that someone's core qualities also house their pitfalls. Someone who is good at taking action can come across as annoying if they overdo it. Someone who is calm can come across as passive. You end up in a pitfall if you use your quality to excess. Keeping this model in mind, you can take a very close look at your own working style. Perhaps you "overdo it a bit"? Transactional Analysis differentiates five working styles, each with its own typical strength and weakness. They are a lot like the differences in style shown by the colleagues who were having lunch which opened this mirror. As mentioned before: the weakness of each working style is the direct result of an overdose of the same working style. This excess usually occurs under stress, whereby we are propelled by our own working style, as it were.

The weakness of every working style is the direct result of an overdose of the same working style

A psychiatrist once said: "A neurosis arises if something that can be done, must be done." This actually applies to all qualities. Once there is an overdose, the logical outcome is the pitfall. The effects for colleagues are often difficult to manage and not every manager can see the core qualities behind the pitfall. In other literature, you will come across the working styles as the negative pole of what are referred to here as working styles. They are called "drivers." You are driven by your working style as if you had no other choice. Having more knowledge about your quality can help you to use the positive parts of your qualities.

TASK

Questionnaire about your personal working style.

INSTRUCTIONS

For each item, give a score between 0 and 8, where 8 is totally like you, 4 is average and 0 is totally unlike you.

ITEM	SCORE	WHAT I TYPICALLY DO:
1.		I tend to wait until the deadline is near before I work on a task.
2.		I like to organise my work area efficiently.
3.		It is important to maintain harmony in working relationships.
4.		I enjoy starting new projects.
5.		I am very good at staying calm during a crisis.
6.		I work steadily and conscientiously at whatever is required.
7.		I am good at seeing the whole scope of a task and showing initiative.
8.		I enjoy encouraging people and doing things to help them.
9.		I plan ahead thoroughly so that I am ready for any problems that arise.
10.		I enjoy having lots to do (even if I complain about it sometimes).
11.		It is important to check so that there are no mistakes.
12.		I am usually more enthusiastic than other people.
13.		I am usually more balanced and even-tempered than other people.
14.		I am usually intuitive and sensitive to other people's feelings.
15.		I can usually finish tasks more quickly than other people.
16.		Sometimes people seem to think that I'm overly critical about standards of work.
17.		Sometimes I make mistakes because I am working so fast.
18.		Sometimes people act as if they resent it when I am only trying to help them.
19.		I sometimes miss deadlines because I find it hard to ask for help even when I have too much to do.
20.		I tend to start several projects but have trouble finishing any of them.
21.		People sometimes complain that I make tasks too big because I consider so many possible aspects.
22.		People sometimes seem to think I am aloof and unfriendly.
23.		I have problems saying no to people even when I already have too much to do.
24.		I feel impatient when people spend too much time discussing what to do.
25.		I sometimes miss deadlines because I need longer to check my work.

To analyse your scores, please see the next page.

Working Styles Questionnaire - Scoring

Step 1. Transfer your scores to the summary below, against the question numbers, and add up each column.

ITEM	SCORE		SCORE		SCORE		SCORE		SCORE
1		2		3		4		5	
10		9		8		7		6	
15		11		14		12		13	
17		16		18		20		19	
24		25		23		21		22	
Total									
	Hurry Up		Be Perfect		Please People		Try Hard		Be Strong

Step 2. Now draw a bar chart of your responses by marking horizontal lines at the score points.

Total score

40

35

30

25

20

15

10

5

0

Hurry Up   Be Perfect   Please People   Try Hard   Be Strong

DETAILS OF THE FIVE WORKING STYLES.

Be Perfect

Quality: Be Perfect people are looking for perfection – no mistakes; all tasks must be performed with the utmost care. Be Perfect people are organised in their work. They look into the future because they wish to prevent problems. Accurate people are those who perform their duties conscientiously and always keep their agreements.

Pitfall: "It takes me such a long time to make my plan just right, that I will probably not finish it, let alone implement it."

Please Others

Quality: People with the Please Others working style are the best team players. They will make sure that each team member's point of view is heard. They are very harmonious and intuitive in their work; they take the feelings of others fully into account. They come across as very service-oriented and co-operative. Please Others people are a pleasure to have around because they are tolerant, empathetic and understanding.

Pitfall: "I want someone else to tell me what to do. You are the manager here; tell me if I have done the job correctly."

Try Hard

Quality: Try Hard people put a lot of energy into their work. They are very enthusiastic in what they do. They can put a lot of effort into new things by examining all kinds of options. They usually don't miss a trick. They are motivated people, who are great at getting projects off the ground. They are at the head of the line when new tasks are being assigned.

Pitfall: "Everything depends on everything else – I can't skip anything. There are so many things I love to think about that I start lots of projects, while I often don't finish what I started."

Be Strong

Quality: Calm and stable – this is the best way to describe Be Strong people. They can handle stress very well, which makes them great crisis managers. They keep going and don't give up easily. These are people with a high sense of duty. They don't mind rolling up their sleeves to do the dirty work. They remain logical thinkers while others are already in panic mode. They are not quick to ask someone for help.

Pitfall: "Who needs a plan? I can get along just fine without one. I also don't need others to help me anyway. I will do it by myself."

Hurry Up

Quality: Hurry Up people work quickly, respond well to deadlines and are capable of doing a lot of work in a short period of time. That is also the most important quality of the Hurry Up people: they can move mountains quickly! Their energy increases when the pressure is on. "Hurry Up" as a working style differs from the others. This working style usually supplements one of the other working styles. It often goes with "Please Others" or "Try Hard".

Pitfall: "I have already finished it. Can I leave now? OK, it doesn't look very clear...., and do you think the timing of the milestones is realistic"?

QUESTIONS

1. What two aspects do you think are the most important in your work?
   - speed
   - accuracy
   - harmony
   - enthusiasm
   - keeping calm
2. For which specific tasks within your organisation could you use employees with the characteristics of one or more of these working styles? Can you recognise the specified working styles in your employees? Do you remember the last time you complimented them on this quality? Perhaps you recognise parts of your own behavioural patterns in all the descriptions. Naturally you possess parts of each working style. If you look more closely, you will probably see that there are one or two styles that apply specifically to you. Most people use one or more of their favourite working styles sixty to seventy percent of the time. You will be able to recognise them even more whenever you are under stress!

DIRECTION OF THOUGHT 2: QUALITY CAN BE FOUND IN EACH REPROACH

Elaborating on the thought about quality and pitfalls, you can learn to look differently at all types of annoyances. There is a big chance that you will be annoyed by someone who has stepped into their pitfall. Now that it is clear that this pitfall is no more and no less than too much of someone's quality, the quality hiding behind the pitfall will also become clear...

- Being annoyed about the aggravating way someone tries to get a project moving, can change into admiration for the decisiveness/energy to revive the project from the dead. The passive behaviour of a colleague can be viewed in the light of their power: the calm they exude at a hectic time in the department.
- You can tackle the mistakes made (again) on the fly by the Hurry Up person by seeing that this colleague is capable of getting a lot of work done quickly. Don't just wait futilely until they deliver perfect work.
- The hesitant style of the Be Perfect person is the result of their power to want to deliver careful (double-checked) work. They will never be high-tempo workers!

- Please Others people are always willing to remain nice under many circumstances, even when working against obstacles and irritated people. Take note of the fact that they are very caring and help them to take good care of themselves as well.
- If the Try Hard people lose interest after a while, give them credit for the enthusiasm they have already put into the job. They were the ones who got the project going.
- No matter how difficult it is to fathom the Be Strong person, don't make it a big deal. And, if you want to give them a compliment, just say something like: "I know that you prefer not to hear this, but I am satisfied with your work"!

Diversity is necessary to manage complexity

Now it is easy to see that teamwork has a lot of advantages. The five working styles complement one another and offer opportunities for achieving wonderful (team) results. Diversity is necessary to manage the complexity in an organisation and the manager needs to be capable of harnessing the advantages of the different qualities. The same colleagues can irritate each other no end and cause a disaster, particularly under poor management.

DIRECTION OF THOUGHT 3: GOING IN OR GOING DOWN?

As a manager you sometimes notice that you have a smooth relationship with one employee and a rough relationship with another. You may be able to talk easily with one employee about work or about how they feel in the new team but you have to keep a check on the time because they will be off on a tangent in no time. On the other hand, it may be more difficult to talk to another employee about what they have been doing and the achieved results. You don't get any further than short, sometimes sarcastic responses. This may be due to the fact that each working style requires its own approach when maintaining a relationship.

QUESTION

Think, do, feel – it is easier for most people to talk about one of these than the others. What about you?

Contact can be made with anyone in a different way about a different subject. Each person has a certain preference when it comes to the first contact. We call that the Open door in this model. Once contact has been made, the contact can be deepened by entering the following area: *Target door*. A third area is an area where someone does not start talking so well. It is better to avoid this so-called *Trap door* when talking with your employees. By focusing the conversation chiefly on Open door or Target door, you will see that Trap door will become a part of the conversation automatically. You won't have to put forth much effort for that.

	OPEN DOOR	TARGET DOOR	TRAP DOOR
Please Others	Feel	Think	Do
Be Perfect	Think	Feel	Do
Try Hard	Do	Feel	Think
Be Strong	Do	Think	Feel

As previously mentioned, the Hurry Up working style serves as a booster to the Please Others and Try Hard working styles.

Whenever you make contact using your employee's Trap door, you will generally notice that the employee will demonstrate ineffective behaviour. They will leave the area of their quality (working style) and will change over to the behaviour that we designated as the pitfall (driver) (see also Mirror 6). If you doubt whether you have assessed the working style and its connection to communication properly, you can go ahead and give it a try. If your employee responds without demonstrating the negative side of their working style (driver behaviour) you have a good chance of entering via the Open door. If you notice that your employee starts showing driver behaviour, you will know for sure that you will have to open a different door to get any further. Imagine for example that you start a conversation with the remark: "Tell me what you will do this coming week. How will you initiate the project"? If the other person starts talking right away and tells you what their plans are, you are on the right track. Imagine however, that the conversation dies right away: the other person becomes restless, looks at the ceiling and puts the fingers of both hands together. Then they say: "To tell you the truth, I am not yet sure what I should do." You are on an ineffective track. Your best strategy will be to try a different door. If you try and respond with: "I understand you need more time to think about a suitable plan. Can I be of assistance?" the other person might relax and be ready to exchange ideas with you. If you continue talking to this Be Perfect person about how they feel about the different options for a plan that they come up with, they will relax even more and will start working on the plan with a cheerful attitude.

In general, keep the following guidelines in mind:

- The best way to start a conversation with Be Perfect people is to ask questions. They like to work together with you to come up with ideas together about the area they know so well.
- Please Others employees prefer that you first focus on their feelings. They first want to know that you place importance on knowing they are feeling good about themselves.

- The best way to start a conversation with a Try Hard colleague is to take the time to talk about their behaviour in a playful manner. They invest a lot of energy in creative behaviour.
- The easiest way to make contact with Be Strong people is to talk to them about your

MIRROR 4: A SOURCE OF ENERGY?!

A wise woman, who was travelling in the mountains, found a precious stone in the river. The next day she met a traveller who was hungry. The woman opened her handbag to share her food with him. The hungry traveller saw the precious stone and asked her to give him the stone. She gave it to him without a second thought! Happy about his good fortune, the traveller left. He knew that the jewel was so valuable that he would have no worries for the rest of his life. However, a couple of days later he returned and looked for the woman. When he found her, he gave her the stone and said: "I have thought about it. I know the value of this stone, but I am giving it back to you knowing that you can give me something that is much more valuable. If you can, give me what is inside you that made it possible for you to give me the stone."

QUESTIONS

This mirror shows how feelings play a role in your daily work. It brings up questions, for example: "How does that work in my case? How can I deal with my emotions sensibly? And other people's emotions? How can emotion evoke movement and how can I use emotions to increase the effectiveness of teamwork"?

TASK

Emotion is motion! Both words have the same etymological origin. As you can see, feelings are opportunities that can lead to movement. Think of an effective strategy for the following (loaded) situations. How would you react to the emotional statement?

1. Visibly anxious Lisa tells her colleague that she is very nervous about her upcoming review. "I am afraid that I will just clam up," she says with a tense face.

   Your reaction?

2. The tension at the beginning of the meeting is very noticeable. The team finally succeeded in realising the proposed cutback task for the coming budget year. Because of this tension it's not easy to concentrate on the agenda.

What is your reaction?

3. While biting his lip, the employee tells his supervisor in a trembling voice that he has had it up to here with being harassed by his colleagues. "I want to be transferred to a different department or I will call in sick...," he says with tears in his eyes.

Your reaction?

DIRECTION OF THOUGHT 1: THE FIVE BASIC EMOTIONS

"Show them what you're made of." With this remark made by bystanders, you are encouraged not to show your emotions or feelings (both words are used here as synonyms) to others. The thinking behind this is that showing emotion makes people vulnerable. That is true. Anthony Robbins (1996) gives a short and sweet explanation of "the problem" that exists in society regarding emotions: people often fear emotions like a virus that attacks us when we are at our weakest. Still the fascination of the power of emotional intelligence has been increasing in the past few years.

The link between the intelligence quotient (IQ) and social success can only be proved to a limited degree. High marks at school do not predict how well someone will succeed in their further life. IQ only makes up a fifth of the factors that determine success in life. A part that is just as important for determining success is how people learn to deal with their own emotions and with the emotions of others. What is emotional intelligence (EQ)? People can experience their emotions in different ways: "I feel tense", "I am going crazy", "I am fed up with it", "That moves me." All emotions can be linked to one of the five basic emotions. Just like all the thousands of colours are "only" mixtures of the three basic colours red, blue and yellow, all emotional shades are mixtures of the basic emotions: anger, fear, sadness, joy and body feelings. An employee who is disappointed usually feels angry and sad. Disappointment is composed of two basic emotions. The manager who notices emotion when listening to a young colleague's success story, may feel both happy and sad – happy for the employee's future and sad to learn that the employee will be leaving the team.

It's not only about the facts, it's also about the perception of those facts.

The basic emotions can be recognised in all feelings. The question is, how do you deal with them? With disappointment for example, you can talk about anger, but also about sadness! The choice you make as a manager affects the rest of your conversation. Only focusing on remarks such as "I feel so strange" or "I am so stressed out" often does not help. The fact that a note is made of the (and, for good reason, communicated) emotion shown is an important first step. It's no longer only about the facts (what happened), but also about the perception of the facts. What significance does the other person give to the incident?

In that last question lies the key for progress! Dealing with perception and naming feelings is an important skill for all managers. Emotions often provide more information about what has to happen than just going through the facts again.

Forbidden feelings

Everyone learnt as a child that some feelings are allowed and others are not so welcome. Certain feelings are simply forbidden! "If you are going to cry, then go to your room"! "Don't you come to the table with such an angry look on your face"! Children quickly learn to replace these feelings with an emotion that is permitted. A child is afraid of their own sadness. Another child conjures up a smile on their face whenever they are angry.

In time, the child is no longer aware of the forbidden emotion. This is why some employees smile when they are actually afraid, while others show sadness when they are actually angry. This phenomenon sometimes makes dealing with emotions difficult.

DIRECTION OF THOUGHT 2: WHAT IS NECESSARY?

It is necessary to have insight into both facts and emotions to be able to solve problems. Questions like: "Can you tell me again exactly what happened before the confrontation you had with your colleague"? and "Explain to me again exactly what happened. Start at the beginning please!" does not help you to gain insight into what is actually going on. These questions are usually not enough. An employee's trembling voice says that there is more to it than just the facts. At that moment it is a good idea to keep asking about the perception of the facts. "I hear that your voice is trembling while you are talking about this. What does that mean"?

Emotions act as a guide. They tell you what people are looking for, what they value and what is important to them

Taking note of how the employee perceives the facts helps to clarify what is necessary to tackle the problem. Emotions function as a guide. They divulge what people are looking for, what they value and what is important to them. Emotions are not viruses. They are signals that clarify that someone needs something. They are the red light on the dashboard: caution, the engine needs oil!

In the case of the so-called body feelings, the signal function is clear. If you are thirsty, you need liquid; if you are hungry, you need food. If the need is recognised, a person takes action to fulfil the need. A feeling of fear is no different. A person who is afraid should think about what the underlying need might be. The manager with an angry employee at their desk can, once the employee has let off the worst steam, ask the employee: "And what do you think should happen now"? An employee who is in tears probably does not need a handkerchief and a glass of water.

They probably need you to ask the question: "What can I do for you since you are so sad"?

Emotion is motion: emotion creates movement

People who need something and become aware of that need through their emotions, derive the energy from the emotion to fulfil their need. We mentioned it already: Emotion is motion! Real enthusiasm about a plan generates a lot of energy from the happiness this enthusiasm brings along. An employee who is afraid they cannot deliver the promised report on time can convert their fear into energy to get to work and fulfil their commitment anyway. Emotions make people move! The slow steps of the chairperson on their way to the meeting makes you think that they don't feel like doing this today. But they are mainly afraid of possible reactions to their new plans. The most important question is, however, whether they will succeed in converting their fear into the energy they need to handle the meeting differently. People can respond in three different ways to fear: fight, flight or formulate. Are their feelings about this meeting the motor for movement or the fuel for passiveness?

DIRECTION OF THOUGHT 3: NON-VERBAL SIGNALS

People often tell each other a lot about their emotions, with and without words. Therefore, being a good observer forms the basis for all emotional intelligence. The basis for this is a choice of words, intonation, attitude, body language, facial expressions and indecisiveness. They are all indications that the subject of discussion has an emotional charge. It is important to recognise and name the signals, because they touch the essence of what the other person is communicating.

The manager should be able to separate their own feelings from those felt by the other person

An employee who is visibly affected, coming to tell you that he is planning to resign, is not only coming to you to tell you the facts. The message can also be: I am fed up! (angry), I can't cope with continuing like this (fear), it hurts me terribly (sad) or I come to work every day with a headache (body feeling). If you succeed in recognising and naming the emotion, you will be able to help the other person. Staying could also turn out to be an option! It is often enough to name the observed emotion. "I have the idea that you have had it up to here, is that true?" Or "If I hear you right, I can imagine that you are also disappointed. Is that true?" The manager must be able to separate their own feelings from those of the other person. It doesn't mean that you can't express your own feelings in certain situations. Sometimes that can put the subject of conversation into a different light. For example: "I am quite shocked at what you are telling me." Or: "It makes me worry about how your future career will progress here."

TASK

Examine what currently affects you emotionally at work. Do you recognise which basic emotions play a role? Ask yourself what you need and what you can do to get what you need. And, make sure you get it!

... AND THE ART OF SURFING

The www.alberteinstein.nl website shows you how the illustrator of this book, Luuk Poorthuis, views the five basic feelings.

MIRROR 5: UP TO HERE AND NO FURTHER?

The Greek philosopher, Socrates, once walked through the streets of old Athens deep in thought. The sun was shining; it was a beautiful day for deep thoughts. Suddenly, a man approached him from a side street and spoke to him excitedly: "Hey, Socrates, listen, I have to tell you about that friend of yours, you know, the friend who..." "Wait a minute before you go any further," interrupted Socrates. "Have you already screened everything you want to tell me about my friend through three sieves before you go any further?" 'Three sieves?' asked the man in a surprised voice. "What do you mean?" "I will explain it to you, said Socrates patiently. "The first sieve is for truth. Have you carefully verified that everything you wish to tell me is based on the truth?" "Oh no, I heard it from someone who heard it from..."

Socrates interrupted him: "Pity. But I assume it made it through the second sieve? The sieve of everything that is good? Do you want to tell me something good about my friend?" The man hesitated: "No, not really. On the contrary..." "Hmm, hmm", muttered the philosopher reflectively. "Only the third sieve remains. Is it necessary that you tell me why you are so wound up?" "Necessary"? No, it's not really necessary." Socrates smiled, visibly relieved: "You are exceeding my boundaries, dear friend: If what you wish to tell me is not true, is not good and is not necessary, then don't bother me with it."

QUESTIONS

How do you find your boundaries at work? How do you deal with them effectively? What do you do if you approach a boundary? How can you handle questions such as "Is this also a part of my job?", "Can I still justify it?", "Am I permitted to get involved in this?" and "Do I really want to?" In other words: how do you deal with questions regarding the boundaries of the things that can be achieved, the boundaries of the things that are permitted and the boundaries of what is desirable?

TASK

"That too!" A real sigh of someone who is approaching their boundaries. Briefly describe a situation from your experience, in which you approached your own boundaries. What was happening? How did that go? Who was involved? How did you notice this was "the limit"? What did you do?

DIRECTION OF THOUGHT 1: QUESTIONS AT THE BOUNDARY

When people are dissatisfied, they tend to go into a state of 'finger pointing'. It is tempting to place the responsibility for this dissatisfaction on others. This is called "external attribution." Sometimes this is appropriate: poor working conditions, unpleasant or not very competent colleagues, an authoritarian boss, difficult customers or a spoilt atmosphere, there can be plenty of reasons to place the blame on others! A good analysis of who is to blame can lead to the responsibility being placed where it belongs.

You have found the right place for disappointment, sadness and anger!

Waiting until everyone else changes can take a long time and leads to strong dependence

But there is also a different truth: perhaps your colleagues, customers, the manager or the government are not the source of this dissatisfaction; perhaps it is the way you look at and handle a certain situation. Thus, it makes more sense to examine your own part in your dissatisfaction. Besides, waiting around for everyone else to change can take a long time and will cause you to be very dependent. Each one of us is responsible for the quality of our own life. The Me Factor is critical to the result. Anyone who cannot shake off feeling like a victim and who keeps complaining, will ignore their own part too easily, thus hurting their own opportunities to influence the situation. A lot of "you" and "they" and too little "ME." A high level of reflective behaviour is necessary and desirable to properly evaluate the Me Factor. Self reflection: daring to look at your own contribution and its effects proves courage and (self) confidence. These reflections are necessary to allow the brain to play around neurologically with prior experiences. At least that moves things in the right direction...

It is not your job as a manager to solve all your employees' problems. It is more important to ask questions in a way that can help the other person deal with their own problems. It is your job to help employees increase their problem-solving skills. People don't come to you to get a (cheap) answer to their question. They come to you because they don't know (yet) how to handle the situation.

It is your job to help the other person to improve their problem solving skills

Asking questions often helps - interested, sincere and challenging questions. Good questions provide focus and a new dynamic (see Mainstream 2).

Here are a few examples of questions:

- What is the reason you are approaching me with this question?
- What is your main thought in this case?
- What new information does this give you?
- What do others say about this in your area?
- What would help you the most right now?

People notice they are at a boundary when asking a question. An answer to the question can enable the boundary to be crossed. The answer, however preliminary, contains whatever is necessary to take another step. Dissatisfaction often means: "I don't know what is next"! Dissatisfaction can be a sign of stagnation in the thinking process. Asking a question can give that thought process a jolt to continue. "I wonder what is next...?" is a question that can resonate in numerous variants, bringing perspective and the desire for change to the foreground rather than dissatisfaction.

TASK

Take another look at the situation that you described at the beginning of this chapter. Can you convert that into one or more questions? What are the questions?

My biggest question is...

DIRECTION OF THOUGHT 2: BOUNDARY VERBS

If you listen carefully, you can differentiate a number of verbs among the many different types of questions people ask "at the boundary". You can probably hear one of the following "boundary verbs" either openly or hidden: must, want, can, may/allow, and sometimes, dare. A boundary question can always be converted into a question with one of these verbs.

TASK

1. Take a look at the question from the above task. How will your question sound if you use one of the boundary verbs?
2. Perhaps you are wondering which verb works the best with your questions. Sometimes it is not clear which verb fits the best. Perhaps this causes some confusion: is it "must" or "want? Or is it "can" or "may"? Or does a deeper level play a role, in particular a question with "dare"? Examine what effect the different verbs would have on your question and reformulate your question five times, each time using a different boundary verb. Which of the five questions produces the best result in this case?

- My question using "can" is: ...
- My question using "want" is: ...
- My question using "may" or "allow" is: ...
- My question using "must" is: ...
- My question using "dare" is: ...

A teacher maintained in a heated discussion with colleagues that it was unacceptable to make home visits to students' homes. He argued that it would affect the privacy of the students and their families. He had thought about it long and hard and was digging himself into a deep hole. He couldn't let go of the question "Is that allowed?" But he forgot to openly ask himself the other questions. His team leader decided to speak with him. Are home visits a must? Yes, it was the agreement that mentors in the lower classes of secondary school would visit their students at home at the beginning of the school year. Could he do it? "No problem," he alleged, "I can do that"! He didn't want to because of the reason he mentioned previously. Did he dare make a home visit? There was a long period of silence that made it clear there was more to this than met the eye. Only once the teacher could say that he dreaded the home visits, could a breakthrough be made and a solution found.

3. It is necessary to ask your question from a "Me-Involvement" perspective to further accentuate the question. After all, it's about you! If you want to feel influence in a difficult situation, it is essential to present yourself as the subject and the director. Thus not: how do you become a good manager, but: how do I become a good manager? Not: what can someone do to..., but: what can (must?) I do to...

Reformulate your question using "Me-Involvement" and the boundary verb that best fits your situation.

My question is: ...

DIRECTION OF THOUGHT 3: FROM EXTERNAL TO INTERNAL

Must, want, can, may or allow? Or perhaps, "dare"? Can a question that first sounded like: "Must I confront this colleague with his unsatisfactory results?" be converted into the question: "Do I actually want that?" or "May I do that?" or "Do I dare do that?" The choice of a different boundary verb places the whole question into a different light:

- "Must" stands for the internalised will of another person or other people.
- "Want" refers to the personal desires and longings.
- "Can" stands for experienced options, competencies and facilities.
- "May/allow" has to do with the question of ethics and agreements made.
- "Dare" indicates how much (self) confidence and courage are present.

Whenever people come across a boundary, the question, "what is going on", often causes confusion. A clear example of this is the colleague with very little self-confidence. They usually say something like: "I don't think I can do that." When formulated like this it seems as though the problem is caused by the existing competencies. But it is more probable that, with an insecure person, the problem is not that they can't do it, but that they don't dare do it. This makes a considerable difference when coaching and providing guidance to someone! This confusion in language often results in all kinds of misunderstandings. This means that the most unpleasant situations do not arise due to "trouble", but due to a lack of understanding, or more accurately, due to not understanding. The colleague who "absolutely cannot be present at the meeting", is possibly concealing their unwillingness. The colleague who is always wondering whether they "should continue on the same course", does not get around to asking themself whether they "actually want to continue on the same course". Another person insists they do not want a progress meeting, when they actually simply dread it. This phenomenon creates a lot of confusion in meetings about our job, particularly when it comes to boundaries. It's the boundaries that make it exciting, whereby opportunities for change arise! The word "dare" can appear behind each of the other four boundary verbs. When people infallibly maintain that they "don't have to do anything", that they "absolutely don't want anything", that they "really can't do it" or that "this really is not allowed", their problem can unfold with further contact. "I am not looking forward to that at all!" said the team leader, who had just asserted she believed job appraisals were nonsense. Once she could finally say that the problem was actually a matter of "courage" a different conversation ensued.

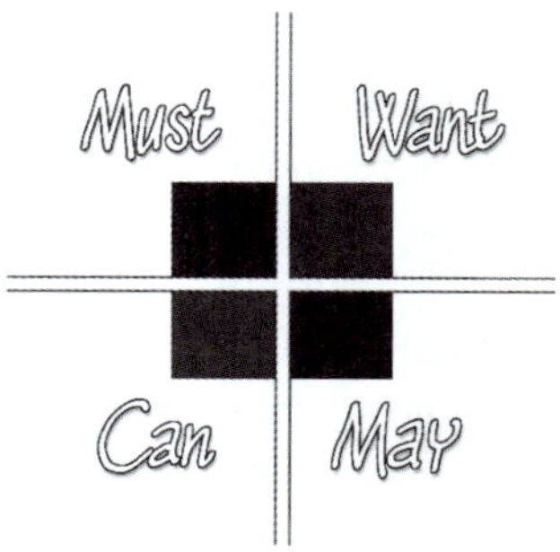

Asking the right question is important for knowing what is necessary to take the next step. If the right questions are not asked, some people will dig themselves into a hole: "I don't have to do anything", "I can't do it", or "I believe it shouldn't be allowed." It is your task to have the courage to give employees a chance, to encourage them, literally: to give them courage!

The quadrant is not a measuring tool; it does not have an exact value. However, it does make it possible to place the experience in four areas in a relationship with each other.

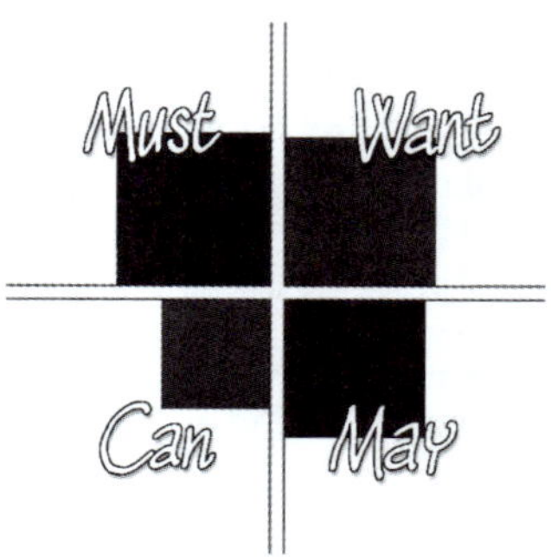

Two important assumptions have been named implicitly for working with this quadrant.

Firstly: all questions must be answered in each situation where there are boundaries: Must I do it? Do I want to do it? Can I do it? May I do it? These questions also play a role subconsciously. Secondly: a quadrant always looks for "balanced" fulfilment. The "must" cannot be stronger than the "want" or the "can" in the long run. It is OK if you temporarily must do something that you don't want to do, because this is how you move beyond your boundaries. It is OK if you temporarily cannot do something that you must do, because that can be overcome. But it's deadly in the long run.

Whenever you start a new task, you often still have to master the balance between the four aspects. In the struggle you are looking for your (career) identity, searching for your internal balance. Wanting to do something temporarily while not knowing whether you can do it enables growth. However, structural imbalance is fatal and creates a lot of stress.

The question of self-confidence is the most basic of all questions

The question: "Do I dare do it?" is the most important question. The part of you that answers this question is the most influential. The question of self-confidence is the most basic of all questions. Each project, each task, each role benefits from trusting yourself, trusting others and trusting in a successful outcome. Time and again this proves to be the decisive factor.

The quadrant is as follows:

TASK

Back to the situation that you explained yourself.

Your question was ultimately: ...

- What makes this question influential in terms of the core of the issue?
- How do the other boundary verbs also play a role?
- How does "dare" play a role in your question?

However, you will probably say that the question has been asked, but what is the answer? Unfortunately, there is no absolute answer. Now you know that you asked the right question, you know that the direction you are looking in is the right one. Moreover, if you asked the question as a me-question, you will notice that your awareness of influence has been given a strong boost. All conditions have been met to find a suitable answer (not the one and only answer). Perhaps you will find more than one answer!

TASK

Name two of your employees whom you manage, who you think struggle with boundaries in their work.

1. How do you think they will formulate their boundary question at first?

2. You know these colleagues well as a manager. How would you formulate or re-formulate their question?
3. What do you think each of them, based on their specific question, needs from you as their manager?
4. To close the circle: if this is what they need, what boundary of yours might you be up against? What question will be appropriate in this case? How will you search for the answer to the question?

... AND THE ART OF SURFING

You will find a protocol on www.alberteinstein.nl where you can boost yourself with a number of solution paths for a current problem in your daily job.

MIRROR 6: WHEN WE GROW UP

The Rabbit family was accustomed to having a lot of parties. A huge number of candles made for a great atmosphere until the wee hours of the morning. However, each party always ended with the same problem: their mouths were not designed for blowing out candles so they had to wait until all the candles were burnt out: such a depressing ending! At their wits end, the senior Rabbit decided to bring in an external expert to put out the candles. At the end of the next party, the expert arrived to blow out the candles. At the supreme moment, he walked towards the burning candles, wet his fingers and grabbed the wick between his thumb and his index finger securely. He put all the candles out in the same way. No blowing! The Rabbit family was perplexed. How is it possible that they hadn't thought of that...?

QUESTIONS

This mirror provides more insight into questions about your personal (life) story. How does your story fit with the story of your organisation? What are the risks of a poor match? Are there also risks to a good match? How do the do's and don'ts of you and your employees keep the organisation on the right course – or not? How does the way you view yourself, others and the world you live in, limit you and your organisation to change and to redefine itself?

TASK

Imagine that you are a famous writer and that you have just written your own life story. How would you answer the following questions by way of association?

- What is the title of the story of your life?
- What kind of story is it? Happy or sad? Triumphant or tragic? Interesting or boring?
- What is the (recurring) theme in the story?
- How does the story end? Explain that in a few short sentences.

The life script is a type of plan of which you are not aware

DIRECTION OF THOUGHT 1: A RED THREAD

It sometimes seems like a red thread runs through all the occurrences and experiences in your life. It appears as though an invisible plan is controlling your life. Eric Berne named that red thread your life script. This pattern in your life, your script, is your best attempt to make sense of the things you observed and experienced as a small child. In this plan lies an answer to the question: what do people like me do with people like you in a world like this? Images of yourself, images of others and images of the world around you influence your behaviour. The life script is a type of plan of which you are not aware.

However, that plan controls your thinking about how you will go through life from birth until death. And that can vary greatly from person to person. The story of your life emanates from the child you used to be, trying to make sense of the wondrous world you stepped into. You assign yourself a role inside that personal story. That doesn't necessarily have to be the role of a hero. If you ever decided to be unpretentious, it can also be the role of a sidekick or the role of a loser, a survivor, a fighter, a rescuer, a destroyer or perhaps a grey mouse. Next, you choose people as examples of those whose script appears to match well with your own script. They assign a role to you in their own story as it were. We will discuss that further in Direction of Thought 2.

There are incredibly heavy elephants at the circus, tied to small wooden posts with a thin cord. Why do these enormous animals just stand there? They could easily break the cord or pull the post out of the ground! When they were young and not as strong, they were tied with steel chains to strong posts that were well-anchored in the ground. The baby elephants would pull on the chain and push against the post. No matter how hard they pulled or pushed, it was in vain. So, they grew up with the idea that they could not move as long as there was a post next to them in the ground. Over time, they don't even try to break loose because they believe they can't.

A script consists of the following everyday content: do's, don'ts, attributions and a programme. Together they form the ingredients of your life story, your script.

1. Do's
The lives of the most famous people are controlled by a number of do's (the drivers).

They are literally the driving forces in life. These do's make it possible to participate in daily social life. People can contribute by Being Perfect, by Pleasing Others, Being Strong, Trying Hard or Hurrying Up. Mirror 3 discusses the positive sides of this aspect of the life script.

2. Don'ts
There is a set of don'ts to go along with the set of do's. These don'ts are sometimes very direct, although parents and educators usually communicate these to children casually and between the lines. These are things that are absolutely not allowed! Injunctions! The

following fourteen don'ts are quite common. Everyone of us has been 'given' at least three to five of them and "lives by" two or three of them:

■ Don't	Anything at all!
■ Don't exist.	You're not wanted
■ Don't be yourself.	You're the wrong gender
■ Don't be a child.	Grow up and behave responsibly
■ Don't grow up.	Always be my little boy/girl
■ Don't be successful.	You never do anything right
■ Don't be important.	You're not a priority to me
■ Don't be close.	You can't trust anyone
■ Don't belong.	You're simply not one of us
■ Don't be healthy.	Be ill if you want attention
■ Don't be ill.	If you're ill you'll have to take care of it yourself
■ Don't think.	My parents know everything
■ Don't feel.	No emotions please
■ Don't have needs.	You don't need anything

These don'ts have substantial negative effects on people's lives. Some examples:

- "Don't do that" leads to a wait and see attitude, thus passive behaviour. Following this "don't" can lead to a lot of complaining. Or fear of making decisions. Or not daring to be assertive.
- "Don't be yourself" can result in people assuming the role of someone else in their life, as if they want to lead someone else's life. They often feel that there is something wrong with them.
- "Don't grow up" makes people stagnate in their development. They have difficulty in taking responsibility. They become dependent upon the Parent system, the managers in the organisation. This "don't" is often given to the youngest child in the family.
- "Don't think" often results in people becoming confused as soon as they have to think about a solution to a problem. You are not doing them any favours by holding a brainstorming session! They would rather be emotional than actually think about something.
- "Don't have needs" often results in rescuer behaviour, ending up in the role of victim! Window 2 discusses these roles in more detail.

QUESTIONS

- Which of the fourteen "stoppers" do you recognise in your own behaviour?
- How do they affect your success or failure as a manager?
- How do you handle that?

3. Attribution

The third ingredient of a script is attribution. Attributions are characteristics that have been developed by listening well to how your parents talked about you. Parents or parental figures in your environment attribute characteristics to you that you will fulfil. "Now I know who I am. I am unmotivated and you can't begin anything with me"! or "They say I am the smartest boy here!" Attributions are used to easily pass on so-called family scripts of: 'He is a real Rogers! You can see that in the intensity in his eyes" and "She is just like her mother - considerate and always cheerful."

4. Programme

The fourth ingredient of our life story is the programme. It is usually the parent of the same gender who models how you should live your script. That occurs by observing and copying behaviour, opinions and emotional reactions. You can be just like him or her "later when you are grown up." All sorts of stoppers are often interwoven in the programme. For example, if the injunction, "Don't be close" is picked up, the child watches one of the parents to see how to become a strong and withdrawn person.

DIRECTION OF THOUGHT 2: CULTURE

How is it possible that one organisation is always successful, while another organisation piles up one failure after another? No matter what answer you hear, the word "culture" is mentioned notably in most answers. Culture is (collective) behaviour! Culture is visible in people's daily actions. No one can escape it. The positive side of culture is that people can quickly understand what is expected of them. Culture motivates social interactions, sets boundaries, thus creating a safe environment. The TA concept "script" appears to coincide with the term "culture." Culture is a system of things that are obvious, based on the behaviour pattern of a group of people that came into existence in the past and that still manifests itself today.

The script is a blueprint for the rest of your life based on decisions made in the past. The organisation script manifests itself in many areas: the nature of the conversations that take place between employees, the clothes they wear, etiquette, choice of words, the way they deal with their customers, social policy and their communications systems. In short, the way they deal with time, money, work and people. We will delve deeper into the phenomenon of Organisation Script in Window 9.

Script decisions are made at three levels:

1. At the social level

This is a conscious decision about the desired behaviour. See decision lists, PR material, reports, handbooks, manuals and the nature and quality of products and services that are being provided. A keen observer recognises here the drivers and attributions of the organisation.

The staff at a nursing home that looks spick & span and tiptop when you walk in the door, are always made to feel they are not doing a good job in management's eyes. It seems like neither of the directors are ever satisfied with the work they do and how they do it. It makes them feel despondent. The beautifully designed brochure that recommends the home, states that there is no other home anywhere that provides such excellent care as this one!

2. At the psychological level

This is a more subconscious decision, often based on emotional reasons. You don't generally find them on paper, but everybody is aware of them. These decisions affect people's behaviour, often without their realising it. The stoppers of the organisation play an important role.

There is a heated discussion at a school about whether the school's handbook should contain job titles. People believe it is not important to specify who does what. "Everyone is equal! Differences are not important", cited one of the deputy-headmasters. No one would even think about entering the staff room wearing a tie.

3. At the spiritual level

These are responses to the question: "Why are we on this planet?" The question as to why an organisation exists has been answered once, often by the founder or by a great helmsman from the past. Parts of the programme have major influence here.

The members of the management team are afraid that the culture process, as presented by the external consultant, will not only have advantages. They can't quite put a finger on what their objections are, but they have a strong feeling that they "shouldn't do it".

Level 2 and level 3 decisions relate more to how well an organisation is faring than level 1 decisions. Social level changes or adjustments are inadequate, for that reason to get real (!) change off the ground. Progress will only be made in changing processes once levels 1, 2 and 3 have been brought in line with each other.

The script (the culture) of an organisation is often an echo from the past. It reflects the way the company's founder or the organisation's pacesetter dealt with people, their outlook on life, their ambitions, their Parent messages and their Child decisions. Organisations which are nothing more than a collection of people with a certain behaviour are characterised by do's and don'ts, attributions and a programme.

It seems as though the spirit of alderman Newton is still haunting the town hall. Sometimes you will hear someone say: "He was a heck of a leader." Nevertheless, there are also employees who absolutely do not yearn for the return of the Newton era. But, the special anecdotes still prevail. "They used to make decisions quickly," many people believe. "Do you remember how he handled the sale of that land back then? Wasn't it great?" However, you hardly ever hear the other story about Newton and how he adamantly and sometimes unscrupulously shoved people aside. He still seems to prevail as a type of untouchable Holy Spirit. You can still feel his influence every day, even after all these years.

DIRECTION OF THOUGHT 3: CULTURE OF AN ORGANISATION

There are numerous classifications of scripts explained in TA. Claude Steiner differentiates three types of scripts that can be easily recognised in organisations. These are scripts in which people become alienated from their basic need for love, joy and knowledge.

1. The loveless script

You will find this script in organisations where employees give each other very little or no positive feedback (see also Mirror 7). Interaction with one another is detached. There are no open expressions of appreciation. People often criticise each other.

Meetings are conducted in a very business-like and aloof manner. The trainees who regularly worked in the department found it boring to work there. They noticed that people talked a lot afterwards and usually spoke negatively about each other.

2. The joyless script

This script occurs often in organisations where there is little or no opportunity for the Natural Child. You hardly hear anyone laughing and there is very little pleasure to be seen. The relationships with each other are worsening.

The firm had logged a considerable record of service in education. A huge offering of knowledge and tools had been distributed to the educational field over the decades. The firm clearly failed in the end due to a lack of passion and enthusiasm for what was really taking place behind the school walls.

3. The mindless script

In an organisation with this type of script, it is practically impossible for the employees to give input and to help make decisions. Relevant information is hardly available, if at all. The result is that many wrong conclusions can be drawn.

The director had his own entrance that led to the 'upstairs office' He held watch there to supervise all his 'subordinates' The upstairs office also contained all documentation, information and literature that could be used by employees to become more knowledgeable. Isn't it strange that hardly anyone ever went upstairs to gain more in-depth knowledge from this enormous wealth of information?

TASK

Examine whether you recognise your organisation in one of these three scripts. Organisations need autonomous people. You can recognise autonomous people by the way they are aware of themselves and the people around them. They live in the here-and-now. Autonomous people always possess more options whenever they have to make a choice. They can determine their choice in freedom. They are open to making real contact. They are honest and open, because they have learnt: people who have nothing to hide, hide nothing. Luck is like a butterfly that frees itself from your grip if you go after it, but will come down and rest on your hand if you open yourself up to it patiently and confidently.

... AND THE ART OF SURFING

You will see an extensive questionnaire at www.alberteinstein.nl to explore your script in more detail. You will also find a different classification of organisational scripts.

MIRROR 7: WHAT YOU PAY ATTENTION TO, WILL GROW!!

A very long time ago there was a boy with bare feet who sat on top of a high wall and looked at the man below him. "Hey signore" he called: "Why are you hitting that stone so hard?"

Michelangelo looked up and replied: "Because there is an angel inside, who wants to come out!"

TASK

Everyone needs attention, some people more than others. This is a biological need. Vitamin L, love, as well as other forms of attention stimulate the bonding hormones, which are necessary to prevent neglect and enable a person to enter into social relationships and to provide and receive emotional intimacy. Also, the type of attention people need can differ from person to person. Each person has an internal thermostat he uses to maintain the "environmental temperature of attention" at the right level. If no one shows any interest or pays any attention, personal growth and professional development will be at risk. This not only applies to managers, but also to employees. In this mirror, the question is: what can you do to motivate your employees? What is the secret the manager can pull out of their sleeve to ensure energy at the right time for the right issue?

Pay attention to something and it will grow! What issues receive the most attention in your organisation? What grows the most at that time? Do you consider that as a positive or as a negative? What do people think about? What is discussed in detail? What do people think is most meaningful?

The following questions will help you to get on track with what is apparently important in your organisation:

- What do people have to do to be successful in your organisation?
- What happens to employees who are successful?
- What happens to employees who fail or only deliver mediocre work?
- Which qualities or behaviours receive recognition? For example, attendance, quality, creativity, competency, seniority, youth, compliance, giving the appearance of being busy, initiative, taking risk, co-operation, education, qualifications, overtime, punctuality.

- What happens when people start work, leave the organisation, get a promotion, or are fired?
- What text is inscribed on the gold watch when people leave?
- What happens with people who stand out, for example, due to their high-energy attitude, caring manner, friendliness, politeness or rigidity?
- What do your answers say about the organisation where you work? How characteristic are these answers for the people who work there?
- Finally, complete the following sentences.

The one thing that receives a lot of attention and appreciation in my organisation is ...

In my opinion that means...

DIRECTION OF THOUGHT 1: BRILLIANT OR DIFFICULT?

As a student at school you can gain the teacher's or headmaster's attention in one of two ways. You either have to be difficult or brilliant. If you are not brilliant and you are also not difficult, you will not receive a lot of attention at school. This lack of attention affects some students deeply. Students feel like they are not noticed, not heard and that no one knows them. They feel ignored. It's not much different in organisations. A lot of time and energy (= attention) are given to employees who do not fit the status quo or to those who are excellent and deliver top performance. There is often a discipline problem with the first group: What has to be done so that they better meet the expectations and where is the limit for under-performing? With the second group, it is mainly a question of bonding: how can we keep appealing to and bonding with the employees who deliver excellent results or an outstanding contribution to the objectives of the organisation?

We can find the secret of treating others and giving them attention in the TA term "strokes". Eric Berne used the word to assign a unit, a certain degree of attention. People need strokes to survive. If they don't receive positive attention (the stroke as compliments, interest, care), people then prefer to receive negative attention (the stroke as comments, arguments, conflict, punishment) than no attention at all. In short: people would rather be "beaten" than "ignored" ("Your outlook does not have a right to exist"). People (and not only children!) who are consistently ignored will languish in the long run

> People who do not receive positive attention appear to prefer to receive negative attention than no attention at all

You can see that a lot is asked of managers. Knowing that everything they do and everything they say is a form of communication (after all, you can't not communicate!), their behaviour and their communication can result in three different effects:

- Negation: the other person feels like no one sees or hears them.
- Rejection: the other person experiences that their opinion is rejected, but notices that someone is paying attention to their opinions.
- Taking note: the other person experiences that someone has taken note of their opinions; they feels they are being seen, heard, and known.

Systematic rejection, but particularly long-term negation, makes employees drop out, become demotivated, leave things as they are, display passive behaviour, become cynical. With "a bit of luck" they will leave the organisation. If not, the effects are counter-productive for both the person and the organisation.

Berne even thought that people were 'hungry'. Everyone has a biological need for stimulation of the senses and a need for strokes at the psychological level (and a need for structure at the social level). People need to be noticed, and not only on the work floor. Taking note doesn't mean you have to agree with what employees say or do. It simply means that, as a manager, you see and point out their effort (which comes in many, sometimes strange disguises).

A lot of withdrawn behaviour, frustration and cynicism in people has its roots in the feeling that they don't matter, they no longer know how to provide a useful contribution. Failure to appreciate effort is a terrible waste for any manager. Employees often communicate in different ways: "see me, hear me, feel me, touch me!"

TASK

- What kind of strokes do you regularly give your employees? Can you give examples?
- Are the stroking patterns in your organisation different for the different employee categories? For men and for women? For older employees and younger ones? For native citizens and for immigrants? For managers and for staff?
- What kind of strokes do you regularly receive from your staff and your colleagues? What recent example really touched you?
- How do employees generally handle your strokes? What reactions do you notice?
- How do you generally handle the strokes that you receive from them? What happens to you when you receive a stroke?
- Do you believe that improvement is needed in this area? If so, how? Can you give an example?

Are you ready for the big secret? Well, strokes in the form of feedback for achieved results form the most important motivators for employees to work purposefully and efficiently! It goes without saying that the strokes do have to be genuine and authentic. Strokes that are not genuine and authentic are called "plastic strokes". Everyone feels it in their bones that they aren't really of any value.

Strokes must be genuine and authentic

There is very little time for strokes in many organisations. They believe that adults don't (shouldn't) need strokes. You will hear: "They receive their monthly compensation in the form of a cheque. That should be enough!" Nevertheless, there are only a few people who work only for the money. "Pride matters more than money", was the final conclusion from research in the business world. Other research shows that important motivational factors are the atmosphere at work, teamwork with colleagues, the attentive way the company treats the high points and the low points of people's lives, company parties, and the way the work floor is managed and how the personnel are treated. "We do it all for strokes" said Eric Berne.

DIRECTION OF THOUGHT 2: A BULL'S EYE?

Strokes come in all shapes and sizes. In the end, people look for negative attention if positive attention is not or no longer available. Anything is better than negation or rejection.

There are four types of strokes:

- Positive conditional
- Positive unconditional
- Negative conditional
- Negative unconditional

The term "conditional" indicates that strokes relate to what someone does, to their actions, and not to who they are! In other words, strokes for behaviour! Positive: "I like that report you created." Or: "I heard that you gave a great presentation." Or: "Your hair looks very nice." Negative: "Shoddy work!" "When will you finally remember that!?" "Unconditional" means that strokes are given for the person themself. Strokes for being! "I love you!" is a pretty (positive) example. The smile you get when you enter somewhere. "I hate you" is a negative example. But also looking away or sighing when you enter a room are negative strokes that you cannot ignore. The strokes you receive for who you are (strokes for being) are worth more than the strokes you receive for what you do (strokes for doing). There is a type of stroke in there that everyone wants to receive. That is a stroke that we are happy to receive, a form of attention or recognition that rates at the top of our wish list. A bulls-eye!

QUESTIONS

- Which stroke do you generally like to receive at work? What are you looking for? What should others say to you so that your day can no longer go wrong?
- Do you know what your employees like to hear about themselves or their work? Which key gives you the best access to their motivation arsenal? Ultimately, what are they doing it for? Give a concrete example for three of your employees. Is there a similar motivator for the whole team?
- Who hits your bulls-eye in terms of your motivation? How? When? Do you have an actual example?

Your personal stroke pattern consists of the strokes you give and receive. Each person builds a pattern to provide for their daily stroke needs. It is no coincidence that you like talking with certain colleagues. It is also no coincidence that you want to take a walk through the department to have a chat after having worked for a couple of hours. It is not a coincidence that you get fed up if an interesting meeting is cancelled suddenly. Time and again a network of people is built that provides the necessary attention. Whether you are a mayor or bus driver. Whether you are the chairperson or senior management or the concierge, the medical superintendent or the person who opens the door to visitors... We all do it for the strokes!

You only notice how important strokes were to you once you no longer receive them

Only once you no longer receive the strokes you need will you notice how important they were to you. Re-organisations or mergers disrupt the pattern of strokes, the network of employee relationships. It traverses their chats, their strolls around the office, their cups of coffee, their department meetings, their lunch and their other meetings, etc. A lot of frustration surrounding re-organisation has to do with this phenomenon that initially seems so trivial. It takes time and energy after the re-organisation – with a chance for mistakes and experiences of failure – to build up a new pattern of strokes in your new department, in your new team, with your new room mates. The well-known pitfall and danger lurking out there is that employees who work closely and for a long time with customers, parents and students, citizens or patients, will go and get their strokes there, outside of the organisation. This can have a negative effect, and can even occur at the expense of perceived loyalty towards the organisation. Managers who are paying attention are a step ahead.

Tom was a perfect employee. As a manager, you never had to bother about him. Never any complaints from customers, nothing more than praise. Always busy with the most difficult tasks for the biggest customers. You would want to have a lot of employees just like him. Until one day, without any apparent reason, Tom resigned and went to work for your biggest customer. It didn't look like he did it for the money... but, why did he do it?

TASK

A number of questions of the conscience to ponder:

- Do you give the strokes you like to give or the strokes your employees like to receive?
- Do you only give positive strokes to a limited number of employees or are you successful in giving everyone the attention they need?
- Does giving strokes possibly play a role in difficult relationships with certain employees? If so, how?
- What can you do, in terms of strokes, to create a better relationship with more employees?

DIRECTION OF THOUGHT 3: THE MYTH OF SCARCITY

Strokes help determine how employees see themselves as a person, how they see themselves in their role and how they view the organisation. Strokes are handled well in a healthy organisation (see Mirror 1) and feedback is given and received effectively. However, in western culture there is a whole series of myths about giving and receiving compliments and advice, which can result in problems with people working together. The myths don't stop at the front door of the organisation or town hall, the school or medical institution. Claude Steiner explained how the myth about the "scarcity of strokes" results in a number of unwritten rules about giving and receiving feedback. The belief that people can only give and receive a limited number of strokes, is a limiting belief, which has serious consequences in daily business.

> There are myths in our culture about giving and receiving compliments and advice

The following five myths form an obstacle in terms of giving and receiving healthy feedback.

MYTH 1 Don't give strokes

Sometimes we don't give the feedback that we should. That definitely applies to positive feedback, because we are quick to think that the other person will become too big for their boots.

Question: Do you sometimes have a positive thought about someone's contribution without actually telling them?

Do you have a recent example?

MYTH 2 Don't ask for strokes

We believe all too quickly that the answer will not be genuine or it will have no value if we have to ask for (positive) feedback. However, someone might be willing to give a stroke, but may feel inhibited due to myth 1.

Question: Are you curious about how you are valued at work, but you haven't asked?

What are the consequences for you?

MYTH 3 Don't accept strokes

We assume that strokes that are given for no particular reason don't have a lot of value. Or they have a figurative meaning ("He probably wants something from me").

Question: When was the last time you rejected positive feedback, perhaps without realising it at the time?

What do you think was the real reason for that?

MYTH 4 Don't reject strokes

Many women think that they always have to accept comments about their appearance, while they would rather be seen as a total person. Men sometimes accept strokes for their power and perseverance, while they would rather receive attention for their sensitivity.

Question: Which positive feedback would you rather not receive?

Do you always have the courage to reject it? Why or why not?

MYTH 5 Don't give yourself strokes

An old proverb "Never raise thy own praise" says a lot about this myth. You are quickly seen as a show-off if you put yourself in a positive light.

"Modesty is a virtue" is another one. These proverbs are full of myths that originated from cultural tradition.

TASK

If you were to give yourself positive feedback (and we would absolutely permit you to do so!), how would it sound? Take your time and share it with a couple of colleagues.

I am proud of ...

TASK

Stroke Myth questionnaire

For each question, indicate a score between 0 and 4, where 0 means *Not at all like me* and 4 means *Very much like me*.

Afterwards, transfer your scores to the chart that follows.

ITEM	SCORE	QUESTION:
1.		If you praise people, they stop trying so hard.
2.		I get paid to do my job so I do not need a lot of compliments.
3.		It is very bad mannered to refuse a compliment.
4.		I am nervous about asking for direct feedback.
5.		It is boastful to tell people what you are good at.
6.		I rely on other people to know what I am good at and make sure I get that kind of work.
7.		I just assume that my work is okay when my manager doesn't criticize me.
8.		I am willing to accept the blame even though it is sometimes not really my fault
9.		I feel embarrassed when people praise me.
10.		People get paid to do their job and should not need lots of compliments.
11.		My performance appraisal has not been done when it should have been but I understand that my manager is too busy.
12.		I feel I don't deserve praise, especially when other people have helped me.
13.		I notice that sometimes people get given projects that I would be able to do better
14.		I rarely see anyone do a job as well as it should be done.
15.		When someone makes personal comments about me, I don't make a fuss even though I may not like what they say.

To analyse your scores, please turn to the next page.

Stroke Myths Questionnaire - Scoring

Step 1. Transfer your scores to the summary below, against the question numbers, and add up each column.

	ITEM	SCORE		SCORE		SCORE		SCORE		SCORE
	1		2		3		4		5	
	10		9		8		7		6	
	14		12		15		11		13	
Total										
		Don't Give		Don't Accept		Don't Reject		Don't Ask		Don't Stroke Yourself

Step 2. Now draw a bar chart of your responses by marking horizontal lines at the score points.

Total score

40

35

30

25

20

15

10

5

0

Don't Give	Don't Accept	Don't Reject	Don't Ask	Don't Stroke Yourself

TASK

Once you have the results in front of you, consider a couple of examples where the rules jump out at you. What is your conclusion about yourself? Where do you think it is time to burst one or more myths?

MIRROR 8 AN INDEFINABLE PROCESS ABOUT INTANGIBLE PROBLEMS WITH AN INCONCEIVABLE OUTCOME?

A famous philosopher once strolled through a beautiful botanical garden. He stopped and stood for a while next to a very special plant. His behaviour attracted the attention of the gardener. He walked over to the philosopher and asked: "Who are you and what are you doing here"? The philosopher stood up, smiled and answered: "I would be eternally grateful to you if you could answer that question for me."

QUESTIONS

This Mirror shows how you can benefit from a number of insights from the world of the coach. The roles of manager and coach are different, but in the role of a manager, aspects of coaching can mean a welcome addition to the repertoire of actions. We see a coaching method of leadership as one of many effective options, not as the only, one-size-fits-all, approach to leadership. It is also essential to ask yourself the question whether, in addition to being that employee's manager, you are the best person to coach them. It might be more effective to let others with a different relationship to the employee fulfil that role. An abundance of questions! How can I fulfil the role of a coaching manager well? Who is a good example for me? Why? What does that say about me? How can I influence the behaviour of well-educated professionals? What thought processes about coaching suit me? What can I learn from the coaches in the sports world to get players to focus? How can that be translated to the office or company environment? How can coaching help to invite, inspire or stimulate people to step out of their comfort zone, to examine new directions of thought and to proceed in different directions?

TASK

Before you start to read this Mirror about coaching, we ask you to first seek out your own ideas and thoughts about coaching. Your own experiences with all kinds of coaches from the past and the present form a picture in your mind of what coaching means. You can take that mental picture and look at new information and ideas that will be revealed to you in this Mirror. Brainstorm (individually) five words that are related to coaching and write them down here.

My five words are:

1.

2.

3.

4.

5.

Which of these words means the most to you in terms of coaching? Why? Who was an excellent coach for you in your past? Feel free to place them on a pedestal! What made them such an excellent coach? What did you learn from your coach that you will never forget?

Based on your example and your row of words, can you come up with your own definition for coaching? Keep in mind: A good and clear definition describes the essence of something that an 8-year old can understand!

Coaching for me is above all ...

DIRECTION OF THOUGHT 1: ABLE AND WILLING!

It is noticeable how freely the word coaching is used, how it is presented as a cure-all for many issues and problems. However, it is not so easy to specify exactly what coaching is, let alone how it can add value. Shall we make an attempt? Coaching: to facilitate someone in the quest to recognise their unknown capabilities! As a coach, you really must believe in them! Otherwise, you will not come across as believable. As a coach, you can't pull a dead horse... The coaching process particularly involves the development of talent (riches!) that already exists in its basic form.

It can also include attention for practicing (new) skills and gaining knowledge. A coach focuses on people's capabilities and contributes to the development of hidden talent. Learning questions asked by employee(s) form the basis for coaching. These are questions about personal development, about conducting meetings, about supervising, or questions about different work situations. They will often relate to situations in which someone wishes to develop a different professional approach.

The coach uses the work area as a learning environment. Live experience is the starting point and end point for learning. This is also referred to as: "coaching on the job". The role of the coach is to observe, give feedback and to give advice (sometimes) on the job.

The coach uses the workplace as a learning environment

Last century, Hersey and Blanchard presented their model of situational leadership. They asked themselves how a manager can deal with the differences among their employees. They used two polarities: the extent of an employee's **ability** to take on a certain role and the degree of **willingness** to perform the task. Two questions always come to mind when determining the right approach: to what extent is the employee capable (ability) to perform the task? And, to what extent is this employee motivated (willing) to perform the task? The answers to these questions result in four possible combinations.

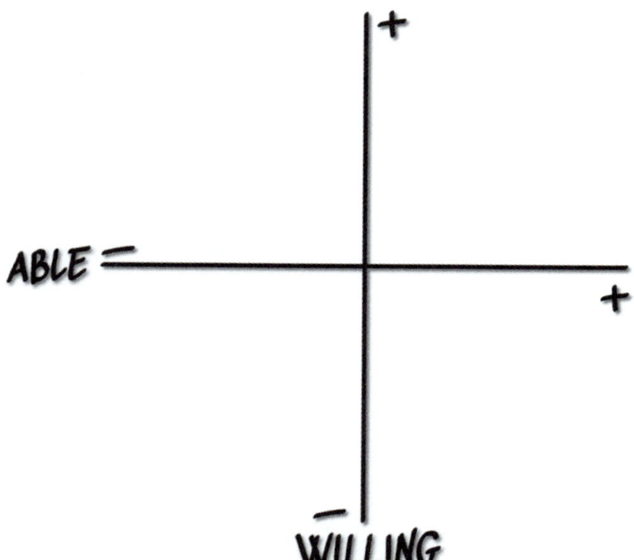

This combination determines the approach to be used. It's as simple as it is brilliant:

TASK

There are four options when determining your input: you can lead, coach, guide or delegate.

When leading, you can think about managing, directing, leading and instructing.

When coaching, you will provide space within clear boundaries: model behaviour and support but also set standards. When we think about guiding, we think about participating, supporting, being a sounding board. When delegating, we think about self-management, letting go, or holding onto something differently.

Take the time to ask yourself what kind of approach your employee needs; beware of the trap of doing what you happen to be good at! Which approach would you choose for each of these employees?

Hamid really wants to do it but he is not (yet) capable. He is a very keen employee. He wants to work on all sorts of things. He is still young and is dreaming of a smooth and easy career. He still has a lot to learn before he can take on some of the more difficult tasks in the department.

My input:

Bob actually doesn't feel like it, but can do it. He has proved that in the past with other projects.

My plan:

Jessica doesn't like many aspects of her work. She doesn't gain any pleasure from her job and is not the most well-suited for the job in the department.

My approach:

Anca can do a lot and is not afraid to roll up her sleeves to get to work.

My involvement:

Many managers focus most of their energy on employees who, in terms of skills and willingness, "should be a little better." The risk of such an approach, that primarily zooms in on people's shortcomings, is that the Ancas of the world, who know a lot and can get the job done, are given too little attention and are undervalued. One (bad) day they end up choosing to go to work for the competitor. See also Mirror 7 about Strokes.

DIRECTION OF THOUGHT 2: LOOK WITH A WIDE ANGLE LENS

Organisation and work are complex matters in which anyone (everyone!) can get tangled up. Individual competencies fall short and people are not always as successful in employing the knowledge and experience of others. The idea that things do not go well (enough!), comes not only from the inside, but is usually fuelled by people in our surroundings who, verbally or non-verbally (or even more vaguely and elusively), appear to make it clear that there should be a different and better way.

Coaching can encourage people and make them confident

Coaching can then be a way to gain a better view and grip of a person's own thoughts and actions, within this complexity of work and organisation. Together, the coach and the coachee explore the issue from different angles, changing the issue while they are exploring it. The change moves towards a feasible (!) reality, not towards a true or objective reality. Being able to look together with another confident person at the questions that arise in your context is encouraging: it literally gives you the courage to continue in a good way. Coaching can encourage people: it makes them confident!

TASK

1. Take a general look at what you are good at in your job and write that down briefly. I am particularly good at ....

2. Then write down a couple of answers to the question: how did you find that out via other people? I noticed that through ...

Coaching always starts with a question. The questions bring about the following:

- Realisation: "What happened to you after that aggravating incident?"
- Differentiation: "Did any colleagues agree with your ideas wholeheartedly?"
- Perspective: "How do you keep going?"
- Broadening: "How do people in other departments view that?"
- Movement (what is the foreground and background of the thoughts and perceptions of the person being coached): "What makes that example so important to you?"

In this approach, the coach is not the expert who knows everything (better). That's not possible, because the coach doesn't see the same reality as the person being coached, since they both have different experiences, different perspectives, and both live in different communications contexts. If the coach does not know it better and does not necessarily need to know it, the coach will obviously ask questions: they will both gain better insight into what is going on. A good fit between coach and person being coached is essential, because the relationship forms a practical vehicle for change. Change is often given the meaning that something is not going well. The individual perspective also plays an important role. We see change here more as a constant factor that everyone has to deal with. The coach doesn't initiate change, but someone uses directions of thought that have been given to them, which offers them a language and linguistic reality that they can use to learn to discover options along the way. The directions of thought derived from coaching are developed ideally on the fly into operational perspectives.

A good coach thinks in terms of abundancy, not in terms of deficiency

A good coach thinks (and teaches others to think) in terms of abundancy, not in terms of deficiency. This coach uses a wide-angle lens instead of a zoom lens. They not only focus on the internal psyche of the person being coached, but above all, they focus together with the other person on the phenomena in context. In the words of Paul Watzlawick in his groundbreaking book. Pragmatics of Human Communication "... a phenomenon remains inexplicable as long as the vision is not broad enough to surround the context in which it occurs." In this system of theoretical interpretation, the purpose of coaching is to stimulate the person being coached to learn within their own context. Thus, it would be handy for you to learn to better understand yourself in that context. It boils down to the central theme of this book: how do I take up my role effectively in this organisation and in this context? This learning process does not initially involve gaining knowledge. Above all, it implicitly boils down to all sorts of questions about interpretation.

DIRECTION OF THOUGHT 3: PROVOCATIVE COACHING

Coaching can be seen as an 'Indefinable process about Intangible problems with an Inconceivable outcome'. In that case, definitions come up short, the problems are hard to pin down, and how will it end who knows? It's all a big laugh. Actually, humour is an important part of so-called provocative coaching.

Provocative coaching forces the other person to make choices. Of course, you will always be able to find someone who will ask you empathetically about your prior experiences and your beliefs. However, all too often, this type of 'service' gets stuck in good intentions, without obligation and 'more of the same'. However, a coach that takes risks, looks for your boundaries and dares to give you honest and merciful feedback, is rare. Provocative coaching is a combination of contact, humour, provocation and free association. An excellent stimulus in situations in which people are coached, advised, mentored and so on. In particular if the serious, well-meaning, helpful style comes to a halt, the provocative style can be a result and a relief.

Jane asked for yet another meeting with her supervisor. She always brought up the same topics in these meetings. Her supervisor could almost predict the start and finish of such a meeting. It usually started with a deep sigh by Jane and it usually ended with a well-meant "We will try again." This time, Jane's supervisor had had enough. He chose a more confrontational strategy. As soon as Jane entered, the supervisor asked with a great sigh: Jane, do you have any idea how this meeting will end? Two baffled eyes looked at the supervisor. Then Jane started to laugh and this meeting took a completely different turn. The pattern had been broken. It was a relief for both of them.

It remains to be seen whether listening carefully, being patient and taking the employee seriously is always the most effective approach. Sometimes it is necessary to push someone outside their comfort zone, to pull them, tickle them, challenge them and confront them. This can also be a form of mercy!

Provocative coaching could possibly work with employees who have a low sense of reality, who are often misunderstood and demonstrate passive behaviour (see Window 4). Many people get into trouble if their perception of reality is clouded or disturbed. Disturbed reality can be categorised broadly in four ways:

1. Everything that goes wrong is my fault.
2. Nothing that goes well is due to my actions.
3. Everything that goes well is due to my actions.
4. Nothing that goes wrong is my fault.

TASK

Do you recognise one of the disturbances mentioned above? Which one(s) in particular? Can you provide examples of the consequences for yourself and for your surroundings? What can you do differently in the near future?

The provoking coach could add with a smile: "Don't do anything. Keep going. It's going well isn't it?" This coach is speculating on the last bit of adrenaline for the person being coached, who will (hopefully) bounce back with energy and affirm that they will really get to work now. The coach, however, will not be convinced that easily. Meanwhile, the coach has succeeded in getting the other person to take the future into their own hands!

FINALLY

Do you want to know what our favourite definition of a coach is? We are inspired by our Flemish communications expert, Flor Peeters, whose thoughts about coaching form the foundation for Direction of Thought 2. He described coaching as "a meeting in which complexity is given the right to exist". The coaching manager searches for the real contact point, the inspired meeting and realises that the questions asked by the person being coached merit being seen and heard in a broad and complex context. That appeals to characteristics such as empathy, respect and heartfelt interest. And, all of that preferably on a layer of common sense!

Coaching is a meeting in which complexity is given the right to exist

...AND THE ART OF SURFING

Maarten Kouwenhoven developed the concept "strategic coaching." Strategic coaching promotes thinking in terms of opportunities instead of in terms of problems. The purpose of coaching is to increase the employee's problem solving ability. There are two aspects of importance for strategic coaching: development of the human axis – wellbeing coaching – and development of the task axis – work-orientated coaching. The website www.alberteinstein.nl contains a couple of questionnaires to gain focus in wellbeing-oriented coaching and work-oriented coaching. You can find ideas there to prepare well for coaching meetings with employees.

MIRROR 9 HAVE COURAGE AND TAKE RISKS!

One of the final English examination assignments at a school for Pre-University Education was to write an essay entitled "What is nerve?" One of the examination rules was that the essay needed to have a minimum number of words. One point would be deducted for every ten words the essay was short of the required total.

One candidate was already finished after just two minutes and handed in the essay in front of a room full of amazed fellow students. After the essays were assessed it became apparent the teacher had given it full marks. That essay consisted of just three words which were: "This is nerve".

QUESTIONS

What was the most recent decision you made that gave you a great kick? What did you do when you took a big risk? What opportunities did you see? Why did you see those opportunities while others did not? What happened to make you really believe in them? How did you include others? Why do you think they trusted your judgment? By the way: have you ever made an error in judgment? A risk that went sour? How did you manage the consequences?

Personality and competencies, as research shows, are decisive factors for successful entrepreneurship. The following five characteristics are key:

- Reflective abilities: entrepreneurs hold up a mirror regularly to themselves (and others). They have a high "Einstein factor," they know how to ask the right questions at the right time. See Mainstream 2.
- Strategic attitude: entrepreneurs continually search for, find, make and take up the role of 'strategist'. See Mainstream 3. Strategists are policy makers. They determine the policy to follow!
- Leadership abilities: entrepreneurs are leaders. Leaders are not only heard because they are the boss, they are heard because they lead the way and model example behaviour. See Mainstream 1.
- Communication skills: entrepreneurs are usually great communicators. They not only focus on their message, they focus even more on the people listening to their message. They ask themselves whether their intentions will have the desired effects. See Mirror 2.

- Courage: entrepreneurs demonstrate nerve and take risks. Being an entrepreneur means taking risks! "Someone who doesn't have the courage to lose can never win!" People without courage are probably on the sidelines. See this Mirror.

TASK

Ask five of your closest employees the following question: on a scale of 1 to 10, how do you judge my reflection skills and strategic attitude, etcetera.

What stands out from the reactions? Are there a lot of similarities? Big differences? Note a number of conclusions resulting from the good meeting you had about the results.

DIRECTION OF THOUGHT 1: ENTREPRENEURS ARE EVERYWHERE...

Leadership and entrepreneurship: qualities that matter, but that have been suppressed since childhood. Education and upbringing often have very little stimulating effect on entrepreneurship, displaying initiative, searching for boundaries and creativity. Schools often consider entrepreneurial boys and girls to be difficult and unmanageable. The adage is still all too often "Adapt, accommodate and join" instead of "Courage, search for your boundaries and.... add." Leadership and entrepreneurship are still too often seen as individual competencies: it's something you primarily possess within yourself or that you can best develop yourself, individually, on your own. We think it's much more complicated. People are only capable of limited self (!) development. They are more dependent upon influences, opportunities, examples, possibilities and challenges in their surroundings for this development. Fundamentally it boils down to the qualities that each human being possesses to a greater or lesser degree. To blossom or even to reach full maturity, an environment, or a broader context of the organisation and the company is necessary to showcase trust in people and to offer full opportunity to develop their own qualities.

You will find entrepreneurs at all levels of the organisation

You will find entrepreneurs in every company and at all levels of the organisation. In the best case scenario, they are recognised and valued. If not, you run the risk that these types of employees will leave to open their own chain of shops (or to pursue a different dream). Thus, entrepreneurship is not just for entrepreneurs!

QUESTIONS

How has your upbringing influenced your entrepreneurial spirit?
What was the influence of your experience in education?

How have examples in your surroundings stimulated your entrepreneurial spirit?
Who was a major role model for you? Why?
Can you see how different contexts have (had) a different influence on your entrepreneurial spirit?

TASK

Compare your organisation with a ship and then ask the following question: Who, of all (!) the people, related to the ship, has the most influence on a successful and safe journey? The captain? An extremely important person on a ship, who has the ultimate responsibility for the voyage. The first mate? We cannot do without this person on the ship either. They know the capabilities of the ship and the waters it sails in. The sailors? No ship makes a safe journey without their efforts. Nevertheless, these are not the right answers. The chef? The ship's doctor? Or...? Ask a couple of your employees what they think.

You will find the only right answer at the end of Direction of Thought 3.

DIRECTION OF THOUGHT 2: A MATTER OF INTUITION!

Entrepreneurs stand out as people who show how it can be profitable to take risks, not only in their own interest, but also in the interest of many, in particular all employees who maintain their families and pay their mortgages thanks to the business. Taking risks is a quality among entrepreneurs, but outside that world, it is hardly considered a quality. It seldom gets you good marks in school! The business owner needs strong communications skills to 'entice' their people to participate in risky business. They often act based on intuition, but because they have to motivate people to join them, they have reports created with facts and figures which give an objective look at their 'idea', so to speak. Conviction and charisma ensure that as many people as possible can believe in their idea. Otherwise, hesitant employees would turn it into a precarious business.

Entrepreneurs have a high Einstein factor

It is worth noting that many large entrepreneurs chiefly speak of their methods in terms of "common sense", "intuition", "a good feeling" and "confidence." They also tend to be people with a strong "Einstein factor." They are good at asking questions: What is my feeling about this development? How is the morale in the company? What does the customer have to say about it? What do our partners think? What are others doing in the market? What are the employees' viewpoints? What new technologies can we implement? Who will be responsible for our upcoming success? Do we have the people who can and want to work towards our goal? What will real success create? What has probably gone wrong if things do not go well?

TASK

Ask yourself who the real entrepreneur is in the company or organisation where you work. How do you recognise things in this Mirror that have been mentioned in terms of behaviour, communication and presentation of this entrepreneur? Which attribute has the most impact in this organisation? What makes the strongest impression on you? How could you add some attributes from this entrepreneurial attitude to your own attitude and skills? Where do you find the most entrepreneurial people in the company? How are they valued? What is their influence?

The entrepreneur with a nose for relevant developments semi-consciously brings up the pros and cons, the important and less important issues. They subconsciously work on opportunities and possibilities, so that they have a solution to a problem at hand before others even start thinking about these opportunities.

The most modern psychological opinions confirm the idea that confidence in the subconscious area of our minds often offers better solutions. The processing capacity of the subconscious mind is 200,000 times higher than the conscious mind. This is reason enough not to place the conscious mind on too high a pedestal, and to trust in and build upon what has been 'processed' continually in our subconscious mind. Entrepreneurs are experts at it! In the US, people are convinced that good and successful entrepreneurs (almost) file bankruptcy at least once in their entrepreneurial lives. It's not possible that the road building of a successful company or successful organisation is one without a few bumps and pitfalls along the way. Managing a business means taking risks! And what happens if it unexpectedly fails anyway? In that case, a real entrepreneur will always say: "Ultimately, it all boils down to the fact that only one person will assume responsibility, and that's me!"

DIRECTION OF THOUGHT 3: EXCEL!

In 1982 a book was published by two former McKinsey advisors titled *In Search of Excellence*. The subtitle of the book by Tom Peters and Bob Waterman Jr. clarified what the book was about: *Lessons from America's Best Run Companies*. In this best-seller about business that sold more than 500,000 copies around the globe, the authors described the results of research conducted into a number of successful companies in their country. Once we remove the American tone from a number of the principles they discuss, we are left with meaningful directions of thought. Just copying these principles is not a guarantee for success by the way, as some of the companies studied later got into diffficulties. Still Tom Peters was one of the first people to establish that the hard side of an organisation is not only made up of numbers. With his quote "soft is hard" he explains that the "soft" cultural side of an organisation is the most decisive factor in achieving "hard" results. They found that all the successful organisations they researched possessed eight attributes. In our words they are:

A bias for action, active decision making – 'getting on with it'.

Close to the customer – learning from the people served by the business.
Autonomy and entrepreneurship – fostering innovation and nurturing 'champions'.
Productivity through people – treating rank and file employees as a source of quality.
Hands-on, value-driven – management philosophy that guides everyday practice – management showing its commitment.
Stick on the knitting – stay with the business that you know.
Simple form, lean staff – some of the best companies have minimal HQ staff.
Simultaneous loose-tight properties – autonomy in shop-floor activities plus centralised values.

TASK

Place the above attributes in order: place a 1 next to the attribute that is the strongest for your organisation and so on down the list until you get to the points for which your organisation does not score as well. Discuss this with a colleague. Why do some things go so well? What influences apply? Why are some attributes missing? What does it primarily involve? What opportunities for change do you see? Actions?

What is stopping us from being the person we want to be and doing the things we want to do? We can write endlessly about this, but let's not beat about the bush. The answer is: Fear! Fear to make decisions, fear to say what we really think, fear to swim against the current, fear to take the lead, fear to ...

Fear in managers can lead to uncertainty among employees, to frustration in change processes, indecision where decisiveness is necessary, helplessness! Whoever feels fear (and what human being doesn't from time to time?) will do well to ask themself: what am I afraid of?

Answer to the task from Direction of Thought 1:

Captains, first mates and sailors with all their qualities and effort ultimately depend on another person related to the ship: the designer! They custom-designed the ship for the voyage it was going to make. Developing and re-developing the organisation is an important task for managers.

EINSTEIN AND THE ART OF SURFING

The www.alberteinstein.nl website contains a procedure you can use to work with employees on a personal protocol. A great way to initiate a conversation about integrity.

WINDOWS

PERSPECTIVES ON THE SYSTEM IN WHICH YOU WORK

WINDOW 1 WE ARE BUILDING A CATHEDRAL

There was once a man who loved to travel through Italy. One day he strolled through a wonderful Italian city. He enjoyed the beautiful buildings, the attractive parks and the wonderful weather. Labourers were toiling in the distance. They were chopping, chiselling, calling out to others, having fun, sighing and groaning. The sounds kept attracting his attention. He decided to go and size up the situation. After a short walk he arrived at a large square. The square turned out to be a gigantic construction pit. Two workers were busy with a large block of marble right in front of them. He got the impression they were splitting the colossus in half. Sweat beads streamed down their faces. He asked the man who was standing nearest to him what he was doing. He answered curtly: "Can't you see? I'm chopping this piece of stone in half!" Since he had the impression that he would not be happy with any new questions, the man went over to his colleague and also asked him: "What are you doing?" The man got up, with a big smile on his face, pointed towards his colleagues and afterwards he put his finger up in the air: "Us? We are building a cathedral"'

QUESTIONS

This window shows the functioning of the teams. This brings questions to mind, such as: Why teams? What is their added value? What is the difference between successful and failing teams? What makes someone a good team member? What can and may a team member still do alone? What is the role of leadership in teams, and how do you lead a team, with the focus on success?

TASK

1. What is the most successful team you have been a part of?
2. What makes or made this team so successful?
3. What were the results of this teamwork?
4. What was your successful contribution to the team?
5. What was your 'added value'?
6. What would your team have missed without you?

DIRECTION OF THOUGHT 1: COMMON SENSE CONCLUSIONS

It's obvious that a team can perform better than individual people. An English memory aid clarifies it: the letters of team stand for Together Everyone Achieves More. However, western culture emphasises individual performance, whereby you are not dependent upon the (lack of) ability and the (lack of) skills of others. Effective team behaviour is not a given. Team success is also not guaranteed! In their pioneering research into effective teams, Katzenbach and Smith (1993) noted a number of so-called common sense conclusions about effective teams:

- **An important challenge to perform gives a team energy.** The question is: what is the challenge for the team and is it challenging enough? The team is not an objective in itself, but a tool to achieve objectives. Teambuilding itself is seemingly senseless if the team does not formulate the challenge it is committed to undertaking. This means that the team must formulate its own objectives related to and within the context of the organisation's objectives.

The team is not an objective in itself, but a performance tool

- **Team performance is best stimulated by a strong performance ethic.** Conditions that promote the team are useful, but they do not guarantee success. Clarity about the objective (related to the needs of the customer!) and the desired results have a positive effect on the performance ethic and the 'direction' of the energy of the team. This means that the team leader has a role in stimulating performance behaviour, and creating a 'holding environment'
- **Individualism does not have to stand in the way of forming a team.** Individual matters can turn out to be a source of collective power. Thus, as a team member, you are allowed to be yourself. Individual qualities actually gain more relief against the background of the functioning of the team. The differences between the team members will be a source of collective power if these differences are recognised and put to good use.
- **Discipline promotes effective functioning of the team.** Is discipline permitted again? In an optimum balance with the 'bonding' factor, discipline is very desirable. Effective teams set the expectations high and take responsibility for the results. A group becomes a team through disciplined action: the team comes up with a common goal, has a mutual commitment regarding the goals it wishes to achieve. A team defines a group approach, develops a high level of skills that complement each other. The team members also take responsibility among themselves for the results.

A team is more than teamwork. Teamwork stands for a pattern of values and norms that stimulate 'good behaviour.' A team is not a chain of values and norms, but a small group of people who concentrate on a mutual objective and a number of specific results it wants to achieve. The team is obligated to work together to achieve the team's objectives and the members know they are responsible for their contribution towards this common goal.

DIRECTION OF THOUGHT 2: ADRENALINE AND WARMTH

There are two matters that are of vital importance for the success of a team:

- Adrenaline: fuel and energy for the necessary performance
- Warmth: a climate in which people do a lot for each other and want to work with each other.

The role of manager is to generate a maximum amount of adrenaline and warmth, with the right balance between the two.

TASK

You manage a team. How is the adrenaline and warmth in your team?
Take an honest and critical look at the current situation!
Give your team a score on a scale of 1 to 10 for adrenaline.
Give your team a score on a scale of 1 to 10 for warmth.
We can differentiate four types of teams in our minds in terms of adrenaline and warmth:

TYPE 1 Team Awful

The team will not amount to anything without adrenaline and warmth. The members of the team are not connected with each other and there is no connection to a result to be achieved. Everyone does their own thing, but it's not clear what that 'thing' is. It's called a team, but actually it's just a collection of individuals. The whole is less than the sum of the individual members. Leadership has obviously not succeeded in adding value. Conclusion: break up this Team Awful or at least subject it to a complete overhaul from the outside.

TYPE 2 Lean and Mean Team

The lean and mean team is completely different. They really go for it! This team is solely about performance. The desired result is first and foremost. Who the players are is totally irrelevant. If someone becomes a victim of the ever increasing workload, that is inherent to the system and it's just a shame. The team is 'cool' and task-oriented, but it's poor when it comes to their relationships with one another. The leader focuses strongly on the members' individual contributions towards the result. There are big differences in rewards and there is a strong hierarchy. Nevertheless, the Team is a team with potential: the sparks are flying; everyone wants to be the best and no effort is too much.

TYPE 3 Country Club Team

The social aspect is the most important point for the Country Club Team. It feels like a hot bath. You feel at home in the 'good old boys network' atmosphere. Team members do a lot for each other, both at work and outside of work. They don't hold each other too responsible for the result.

("You win some, you lose some!"), conflicts are avoided and there are always circumstances where the established objectives are not met. As long it doesn't adversely affect the good atmosphere. Imagine that someone should fall overboard! The same monks wear the same caps; the underlying differences are washed away and everyone "deserves" the same amount. Nevertheless, Country Club is a team with potential: Everyone receives attention and is appreciated; there are no big egos to get in the way, and the working atmosphere is full of opportunity.

TYPE 4 Dream Team

The Dream Team contains the right combination of adrenaline and warmth. The team members are well-connected with each other and have a maximum connection with the results to be achieved. The objective is clear and is shared among all members. The challenge gives the team the energy to perform together, whereby everyone's part is different and is evaluated on its merits. Leadership stands out by maintaining a healthy balance between support (warmth) and control (adrenaline). The leader is genuine and autonomous and does not play games.

It is pictured in a quadrant as follows:

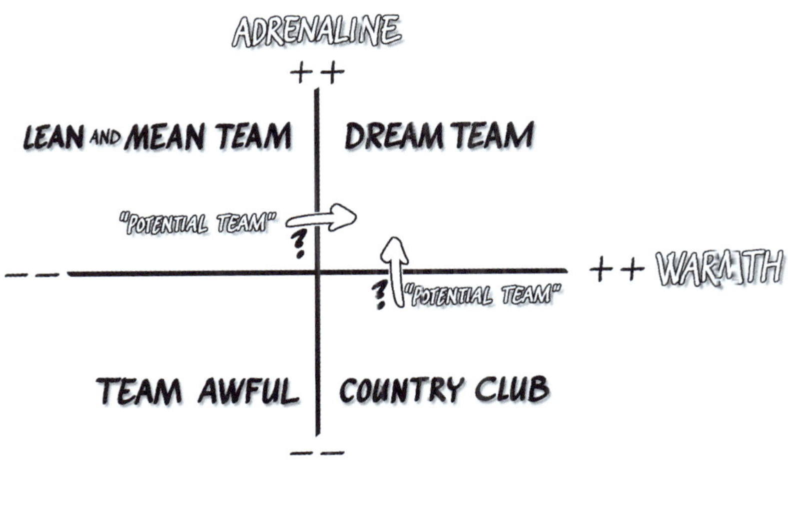

TASK

If you look at your own team, how does your previous evaluation fit in this quadrant? What kind of team do you lead?

If you notice you are leading Team Awful, it's time to bid farewell, because you are not going to solve anything (anymore). If you don't (yet) have the Dream Team, but you do have a potential team, what is the most important thing you have to do for that team?

If you manage a Lean and Mean Team, it is high time to increase the "functional warmth." Your behaviour will serve as an example.

- You pay attention to team-oriented behaviour.
- You explicitly express your appreciation if someone sacrifices themself for others.
- You stand close to the "players" and speak their language.
- You notice if one of the employees is not doing well.
- You are known for your genuineness, your honesty and your autonomous behaviour.

If you manage a Country Club, you can also go for gold. As their manager, you can do the following:

- You provide consistent direction to the agreed objectives.
- You speak to team members about their willingness and competence.
- You strongly push towards the "what": results, contributions and expectations.
- You stimulate employees to improve their individual knowledge, skills and attitudes for the benefit of the team.
- You redefine discipline as "normal behaviour" and require it of all team members.

While taking steps in the right direction, take some time to evaluate the status. Is the whole stronger than the sum of the individuals? And, if appropriate, make sure there is often something to celebrate!

DIRECTION OF THOUGHT 3: YOUR FIRST TEAM!

Right after being born, a person becomes a part of their first team, called "family." Anthony Robbins believes that the family you grew up in is "the first team you were on!" That is where you experienced group membership for the first time and where you learnt your first teamwork skills. Or not. If everything goes well, your family provides you with protection and identity. You will sometimes hear: "You are one of ...!" "You are a real ..."

The family you grew up in was the first team you were on!

The family is not an island. It is imbedded in a network of formal and informal groups in society: schools, churches, friends, political movements, sports clubs and other leisure time groups. Starting as a child, you participate in all sorts of groups. The images you have formed from functioning in those groups determine how you will view groups when you are older and how you will behave in groups as an adult.

TASK
Create a simple figurative or abstract drawing of your family themed: "My first team!"

My first team:

What stands out initially? What (and who) is in the foreground? What (and who) is in the background? Which details have special meaning? What was (is) your role on this team? What else is important to know about this first team?

GROUP IMAGO

The group structure is an important factor for the continuation and effectiveness of the group. Eric Berne differentiates between the public and the private structure of groups (and organisations). The public structure is what everyone perceives, usually on paper (1). Who are part of the group? Where is this group located? How often do we meet? What is the group's objective? What results does the group intend to achieve? The private structure is much less visible and only exists in the minds of the group members. Nevertheless, the images these individuals have of their group or organisation determine what will and will not happen! The private structure is what plays in the group members' minds in terms of their attitude to the other group members and the group leader. The (private) images they have of the different group activities (towards the outside), and of the group processes (towards the inside), influence the development (or stagnation!) of a group. Berne spoke of four phases in the "group imago." A group imago is a realm of thought that each group member upholds (consciously or subconsciously) about what the group is or should be. These images will influence the behaviour in any group you are or will become a member of.

Phase 1 The provisional group imago

People have prior expectations of what the group will be like. These expectations are based on fantasies about groups and prior experiences with groups. The mental image contains

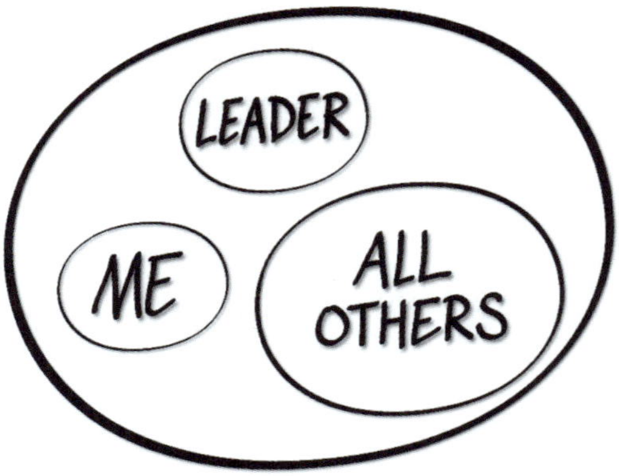

three areas: an area for oneself, an area for the group leader and a larger, still undifferentiated area for everyone else. A person's own area is filled with experiences, expectations, facts and opinions about groups in general and about this group specifically. The area for the leader contains all sorts of images of authority figures the person has ever met, myths about leadership, rumours and fantasies about this specific leader. The area for the other group members can be somewhat differentiated or it can actually be undifferentiated. This depends on whether the person in question already knows one or more members. Images of how the members a person knows behave fill in the areas that are reserved for them. The members they don't know will remain in a large undifferentiated area throughout the whole picture of the provisional group.

TASK

- Sketch an image of a provisional group that you are a part of. Do you still know which images you had when you entered? What were the expectations about the objective for the group at that time? What were the expectations about how the group would develop itself?
- What did you do with these images at that time? How did they affect the content and the nature of your interventions?
- What would you prefer to have done differently in retrospect?

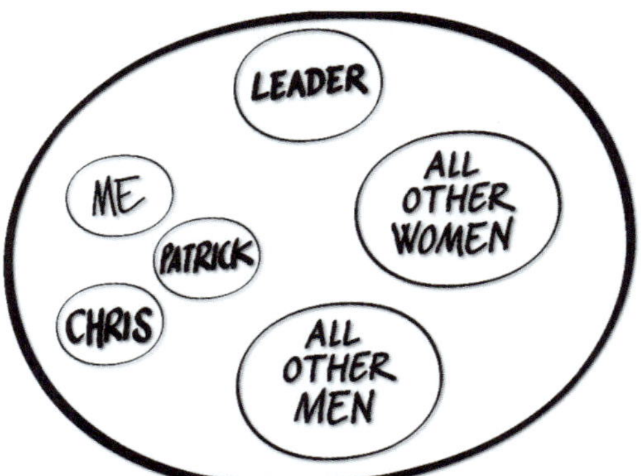

Phase 2 The adapted group imago

The first acquaintance with the reality of the group that a person will become a part of will result in image modifications about the group. Conflicts can generally occur during this phase. These are primarily interpersonal issues: it becomes apparent who else is in this group. The person can like that or not! Resistance can occur against the influence of the group or against the tasks the group will perform. Impressions about other group members and the group leaders will change the group image. There will be undifferentiated areas available for the members that still cannot be placed. This phase is crucial for the development of the group and forms the biggest challenge for the manager.

QUESTIONS

- What do you still remember about this phase? Were there, and are there still conflicts or minor squabbles? What did you notice? What did you do? How did you handle the difficulty or the resistance that was present in terms of the group's objective?

- What would you prefer to have done differently in retrospect?

Phase 3 The operative group imago

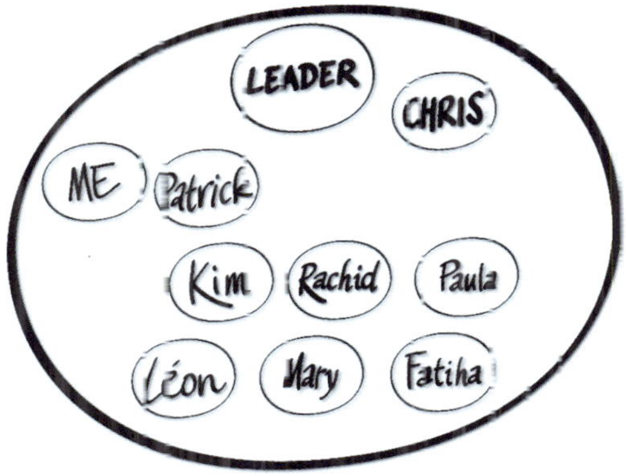

Everyone modifies their imago of the group even more during this phase. This mainly takes place based on the perception of how a person believes they will fit in the image that the manager has about the group. The questions that are on the group members' minds concern the relationship with the leader. From that point, the decisions develop about the relationships with the members of the group. There can be some push and pull in groups during this phase, with an eye on the future pecking order. The resistance slowly diminishes and the group comes together. The group develops its own set of rules This is how we will be a group together!

TASK

- See if you noticed whether group members were looking to see what their relationship should be with you, their manager. How did you notice that? What did you do with that knowledge?
- What would you prefer to have done differently in retrospect?

Phase 4 The secondarily adjusted group imago

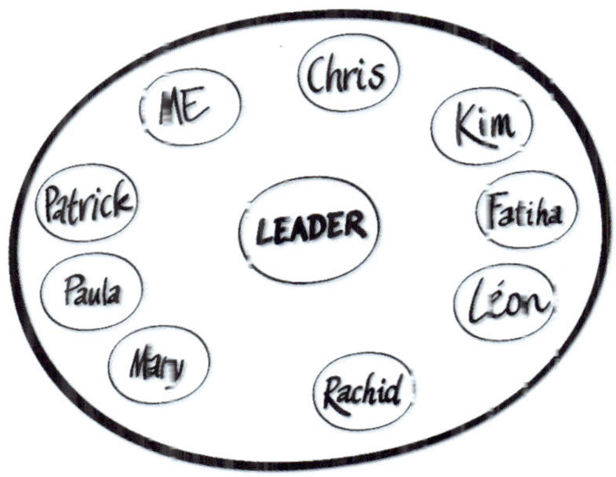

In this phase a part of one's personal needs and desires is 'set aside' to reinforce the cohesion of the group. The group, the continuation of the group and the group success are now more important than promoting a person's own favourite topic. The group gets to work and starts working on its objective. A group that reaches this phase has left "all the fuss" behind and started its work. Each person has already decided which other group members they will hang around with the most, who is tolerable and who they wished were not in the group. The relationship with the leader that works for the team has also been established.

QUESTIONS

Can you see if and how the group you are performing this task for has reached or will reach this phase? Has this group really started its task? If so, how can you tell? If not, what went wrong in prior phases? How can you still rectify the situation based on the knowledge you have gained from this Direction of Thought?

... AND THE ART OF SURFING

The www.alberteinstein.nl website will provide you with an option to analyse your team in detail regarding the question of whether adrenaline or warmth should be added.

WINDOW 2: IT'S ALWAYS LIKE THIS HERE!

The people rescuer didn't answer. His eyes were looking sternly out the window, his nostrils were vibrating. I followed his expression. There was an elderly man walking in the bend in the canal. He suddenly slipped and fell into the canal for no explainable reason. The people rescuer smiled, removed his medals, took a hook off the wall and ran outside.

QUESTIONS

What makes some occurrences so predictable?

Why do certain interaction patterns keep repeating themselves? Why do you keep playing 'games', even though you know deep down that you don't gain anything that way? How do you close this energy leak? How can 'healthy' interaction patterns have a chance to succeed?

TASK

Do you recognise similar situations in your own job? Patterns that seem to keep repeating themselves? The outcomes of occurrences you can predict in advance? How does such an occurrence unfold that you experience as being unsatisfactory? Think about it in terms of a TV or film script: What images do you see in front of you?

- Reflect on the following questions:
- What is it about each time?
- How does it usually begin?
- What happens next?
- (Secret question)
- And then?
- (Secret question)
- How does it end?
- How do you feel in the end?
- How do you think the others feel or felt?

Now answer the "secret questions." The secret questions are:

- What was your secret message to the other person?
- What was their secret message to you?

DIRECTION OF THOUGHT 1: GAMES

"OK, I was just trying to help!", "Why am I always the fall guy?", "Why do I always have to experience this?", "The project would have been successful if Peter hadn't been sabotaging it the whole time – he's always making a mess of things. I'll teach him"! Do you recognise these statements? Do you hear them often at your place of work? They are statements that can indicate games are being played in your organisation. Team members who play games do things like: always knowing better, always whining, suddenly falling out, or making comments at a distance. This behaviour takes place at the expense of the quality and the result of the work. Actual issues are not handled and real problems are not being resolved. Everyone becomes involved in games from time to time. That often takes place without realising it. Sometimes, someone throws a piece of bait out there to start the game: "Hey, what do you think of our new colleague"? Or, "That piece about the director in the personnel bulletin: that surely made an impression"? You can feel the game in the air. An invitation is enclosed in a diversion: to Persecute or to Rescue. Each game also has a Victim (V). The Victim (V) and the Rescuer (R) have a symbiotic relationship, which means that one cannot survive without the other. The third role in the game is the Persecutor (P).

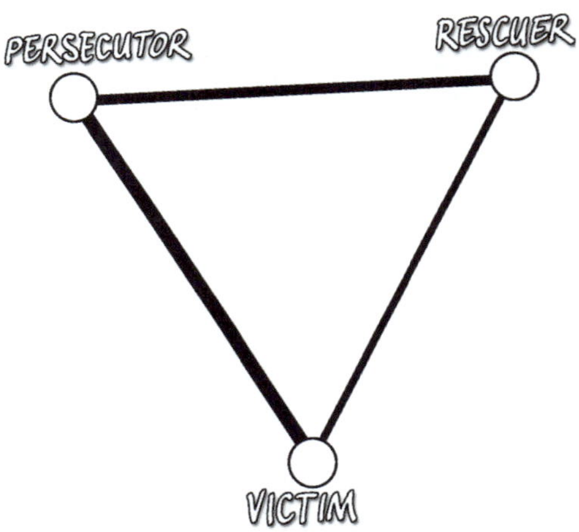

The Drama Triangle or the Karpman Triangle, named after Stephen Karpman, who described the three roles, clarifies the underlying dynamics in a game. The drama triangle is a tool to analyse what occurs in game situations and what is necessary to break away from the energy draining game. What does this drama triangle game look like?

GAME (PREFERABLY NOT LIKE THIS!)

During the department meeting, some employees have no eyes or ears for their manager. John demonstrates that it doesn't interest him in the least. Carla continually clears her throat pretentiously and purposefully. Paul is as critical as ever before. Miriam is using non-verbal cues to show her dissatisfaction. The behaviour of the employees appears to be a big Persecution of department supervisor, George, who then feels like the Victim. They are using this to let him know that he is a failure as a manager. Later in the day he speaks with his sector director, Alice, about it. "The energy in this team has completely disappeared. I feel like they don't take me seriously," he Victimised. Alice, who as the director has all the characteristics of a Rescuer, decides to have "a serious talk" with the "unwilling" team.

That meeting got completely out of hand. The director, who wanted to Rescue the department supervisor, turned out to be the Persecutor to the employees. They were first the Persecutor of their manager and now they feel like the Victim of the director. Department supervisor, George, then stated at the next meeting that he didn't mean it the way the director had communicated it. George wants to be the Rescuer for his employees. He casually indicates that everyone knows that the director is not a great communicator. So, now he Persecutes about Alice. Paul interrupts him quickly and is irritated: "I think that a certain amount of respect for our management can be expected of you"! A new Rescue, a new Persecution. And the beat goes on...

There is also a fourth role in the drama triangle. That is the role of the Bystander(s). Where were Kelly, Samir, Ken and Jeanette when this was taking place in their department? It looks like (!) they have left the playing field and have initially taken their place comfortably in the stands as spectators. From this, apparently, safe place, they do indeed influence the game. Their presence reinforces the game: after all, what is a game without spectators? Besides, they anonymously and regularly throw a cushion or a rotten tomato onto the playing field in a move to Rescue or Persecute. The influence of the Bystanders offers a surprising perspective on team processes. Window 3 shows what Bystander behaviour consists of and what options are available to invite people to join in (again).

There are all sorts of reasons why organisations can be full of games. What are people avoiding by resorting to the game? The common thread in all possible answers is: games are played out of fear of the real encounter! People play to avoid what will be said, what is really wrong, because they dread entering into a conversation about the root cause of the problem. People are afraid of the vulnerability that is associated with real contact.

Games are played out of fear of a real encounter!

What is actually stopping the department supervisor, George, from expressing his feelings openly and honestly to his colleagues? He could say: "I don't feel like I am being heard. That bothers me. I want to consult with you and work with you better." And why is it so difficult for the employees to give their supervisor the feedback that he probably deserves? An additional "advantage" for the players of the game is that it reconfirms their image of the world. Looking back at a game, the players say to themselves, and sometimes to others, something like "It just goes to show yet again that..." This is how they make sure that the world around them always fits their existing image of the world. If reality actually differs from the reality in their minds: too bad for reality! A department manager talking about his employees: "They never listen"! The employees talking about the department manager: "He still doesn't get it"! The director: "I always knew he wouldn't make it"

DIRECTION OF THOUGHT 2: I TOLD YOU SO-ISM

People have a tendency towards retaining their own view of the world. This can be seen as first, second and third degree "I Told You So-ism." You can hear it in statements like "They never listen to me", "He doesn't know anything about it", "Alicia always does what she wants." Words like "never", "nowhere", "always" and "nothing" indicate that the nuance has been lost. The facts no longer help to convince someone to the contrary. However, reality is seldom that clear and monocausal. Of course there are times when employees do listen. The other person obviously knows something about it occasionally! Even Alicia sometimes tells another person's tale. Over-simplified use of language is typically an I Told You So-ism. Especially in terms of third degree I Told You So-ism (game) the facts no longer help. We will explain the three degrees of "I Told You So-ism" here.

1. Selection: selective observation results in signals being picked up easily that match what the person was already thinking. 100 billion brain cells select what suits us the best from 10,000 sensory stimuli per second. This can lead to first degree I Told You So-ism. A person can hold onto their own opinions about themself, about another person and the world, even for a lifetime. I told you so!
2. Interpretation: second degree I Told You So-ism not only uses selective observation, it also makes sure that existing thoughts do not have to be adjusted by 'incorrect interpretation'. If someone already believes that managers never listen to their employees, the encounter with a manager who does express interest, can lead to confusion. In that case, you can 'decide' to not notice that interest. You can also interpret it freely: "Well, it seems like they're listening, but they aren't really listening because they already came up with their own plan a long time ago. That's how they are"! I told you so!
3. Manipulation: in case of a first or second degree I Told You So-ism, it can sometimes help to add information and to go through all the facts again. In this way, you can show that a certain opinion, at least for this situation, does not mesh with reality. This no longer helps for a third degree I Told You So-ism. This case not only involves 'selection' and 'interpretation', but especially "manipulation." This manipulation, by being a Victim, Rescuer, Persecutor or Bystander, invites the other person to display behaviour whereby the 'player' can hold onto their thoughts.

Both colleagues thought: "Our manager is an awfully miserable person." What they could no longer see was how they used their own behaviour to manipulate their manager into this irritable and hostile attitude. I Told You So!

TASK

Can you see a form of third degree I Told You So-ism in the example of the department meeting in Direction of Thought 1? What is the department supervisor telling himself? And what about the team members? The director? The bystanders? The 'advantage" of I Told You So-ism is that as long as the image of reality does not have to be adjusted, it is not really necessary to change! You don't have to move! Again: games are usually played due to fear of the real encounter, fear of saying what is really on your mind. Many things remain unspoken this way. Emotions remain hidden. Actions do not get off the ground. You can have the illusion you are safe in the ivory towers of your own beliefs. Apparently invulnerable!

DIRECTION OF THOUGHT 3: DEALING WITH THE AVAILABLE TIME

Games can be over quickly or they can last a long time, from a couple of minutes to years and years. The effect is always negative in the long run. In the end, all players are left with a bad taste in their mouth. ('Yuck, I feel awful as usual after our weekly meeting"!) The third degree game even causes permanent damage. Games are rather counter-productive for organisations. Employees who should be focusing their energy on finishing a job, completing a task, making decisions, resolving problems or simply performing their daily duties, become mixed up in all sorts of games that eat up time and energy. Games are a way of structuring time.

That makes it even more appealing, because structuring time is a basic need for every human being. Boredom causes mental and physical decline over time.

TASK

What does your work day look like? How much time do you spend on:

- Daydreaming, separating yourself and thinking about things that have very little to do with work (withdrawal)
- Set habits and conventions that have to take place every day (rituals)
- Chatting, having fun, gossiping (passing time)
- (Together) working on tasks that have to be completed (doing things together)
- Feeling good about a special meeting or conversation (encounter)
- Feeling bad about yourself and others (game)

Berne's model of time structuring mirrors the complexity that sometimes characterises relationships at work. According to Berne, the model provides insight into what extent people allow themselves to be involved in a work relationship and in the intensity of strokes (see Mirror 7), which are exchanged in every working relationship.

Withdrawal

People sometimes withdraw physically and mentally. There can be all sorts of reasons for this. You might have a need to think quietly about things. You may need to distance yourself from an escalating conflict. Stress can make it desirable to take a break, to retreat, to be by yourself, alone; complete relaxation can be healthy and useful. It can also have an aggravating reason, such as the lack of ability to have a real encounter. Instead of saying what you want to say or what needs to be said, you choose the safe route of separation.

Rituals

A ritual is a socially programmed time expenditure, in which everyone knows what he or she has to do. Organisations are often characterised by a typical set of routines and rituals. If you enter and say "Good morning"! It doesn't appear to be anything special. Until one day, the usual answer no longer sounds. Only then will you realise the value of the ritual. Overly cliché-like behaviour occurs at the expense of the real encounter!

Passing time

Killing time occurs by using each other's time to talk together about unimportant subjects, such as the weather, traffic, sports, cars and clothes. Killing time is a relatively safe and polite way of making contact. It is well-suited for people who do not know each other that well, since there is not much risk that it will become tense.

Chitchat is a very special form of killing time: chatting, talking, having a conversation. This is usually not valued much at work, especially in this current no-nonsense period of rationality, measurability, manageability, management and transparency. However, it is a good and very healthy way for people to exchange standpoints and directions of thought casually and informally. Chitchatting a while about yesterday's difficult meeting with a colleague or with a group at the coffee pot can be very healthy to assess people's (preliminary) opinions. Chitchat helps people deal with the complexity of what they are experiencing. The line between chitchat and game is drawn where damage is inflicted upon others.

Activities

When undertaking activities (together), these should be objective matters, such as projects that you want to get off the ground together. The result can be gratifying. The process itself can also be interesting. Writing a report together is an example; going through ideas with a colleague and setting up and holding a meeting to discuss these ideas is another example. Activities provide a lot of satisfaction, but they make you more "vulnerable" than withdrawal, hanging onto rituals and wasting time. Once a project that you have enjoyed participating in has been completed, it can be followed by a 'black hole.' Now what?

Game: Always a negative outcome

Playing games is an entirely different matter: hidden agendas, manipulation and painful results. People play games for a temporary release from not feeling OK about themselves, and to avoid having to deal with reality. This puts the game on the opposite side from the encounter. The 'profit' is attention, attention and attention. See Mirror 7: Strokes. The 'loss': having a bad feeling about yourself and others.

Encounter: Always a positive outcome

An encounter boils down to direct expression of meaningful ideas and feelings without holding back. This real contact is not so easy. Too much openness often invokes mistrust and can lead to abuse. The lasting effect of a real encounter is often more than worth it: performing interesting tasks together, experiencing exciting times, achieving a deep working relationship.

ENCOUNTER (IF AT ALL POSSIBLE: LIKE THIS!)

Department supervisor, George, had been noticing a certain degree of dissatisfaction with a number of team members for some time now. He had carefully observed them during the past two meetings. It was now high time to finish the job. He decided to have a chat with his director, Alice, about it. He knew Alice well; he trusted her and Alice would not spare him for his part in the issue. An open, respectful and confrontational meeting about the issue provided George with a number of options to embrace the issue. "In any case", he thought, "I want our team meeting to continue to be the focus of our duties. That's where it all must take place. I will take the time to look at how I can be better and more effective!"

George first decided to conduct short, one-on-one meetings with all (!) employees under the motto "What is going well and what improvements can be made?" Those meetings provided him with a surprising wealth of information about how they viewed the meetings. He also heard a lot of useful feedback about his own role as chairman.

He accepted the suggestion to ask Samir to chair the meeting. He was great at it, as had been noticed once when George was absent. Besides, George could contribute more to the content. He also accepted the idea of preparing the agenda with two other colleagues so that there was more involvement. He also accepted John's offer to write the decisions on the flipchart. Looking back on the meetings, he realised that, although they didn't spare him, everyone showed they were ready to look at their own input and contribution. He had made it clear to them that he appreciated that. Of course he stopped by at Alice's office, but she was not there. Therefore, he left a card on her desk with the text: "Dear Alice, Thank you for your feedback. I needed it. My team responded wonderfully to the meetings. Perspective for the future"!

Karpman (1968) basically considered ten percent of each role in the Drama Triangle to be OK. The intentions are often good, but things often go southsour? afterwards, because:

- The Victim is looking through window I- YOU+ and discounts their own ability to solve problems.
- The Rescuer is looking through window I+ YOU-, and discounts the other person's ability to solve their own problems.
- The Persecutor is also looking through window I+ YOU-, and thinks they can only feel good once the other person has paid the price.

Thus, it is a matter of paying attention so that you keep looking through the "I'm OK, You're OK" window. This prevents gamey behaviour. That does not mean that you always have to approve the other person's behaviour; but it does mean you can continue to fully view the other person as someone who can think independently, who is reflective and creative, and who is worth loving. Based on an idea by Acey Choy (1991), the opposing, positive roles of the Drama Triangle are mentioned below in the Winners' Triangle:

- Instead of being the helpless Victim, allow yourself to be vulnerable.
  You take responsibility for your own thoughts, feelings (and needs!) and behaviours.

- Instead of being the Rescuer, offer your caring abilities.
  You make clear agreements with the other person about what they can contribute. You don't do any more or any less than has been agreed.

- Instead of being the Persecutor, your assertive way of working keeps your own interests and the other person's interests in mind. You say what you think, believe and feel without hurting the other person.

TASK

We are making seven suggestions to avoid a Game.

1. Recognise and acknowledge that you have entered the drama triangle: you cannot change what you don't acknowledge.
2. Do not exaggerate your own abilities or lack of abilities. Also, do not exaggerate the other person's abilities or lack of abilities
3. Do not manipulate others by persecuting or by rescuing them.
   Don't let others who are playing the helpless victim manipulate you either.
4. Do not give negative attention to others; instead tell them what you value.

5. Spend your time on healthy and open relationships instead of wasting time on all sorts of political and strategic games.
6. Stop wasting energy on things that you believe are negative.
7. Allow yourself to think that it's OK to enjoy your life and your job.

Which tips do you think you will use? How will you use them?

... AND THE ART OF SURFING

The www.alberteinstein.nl website contains a summary of the games that frequently occur in companies and organisations.

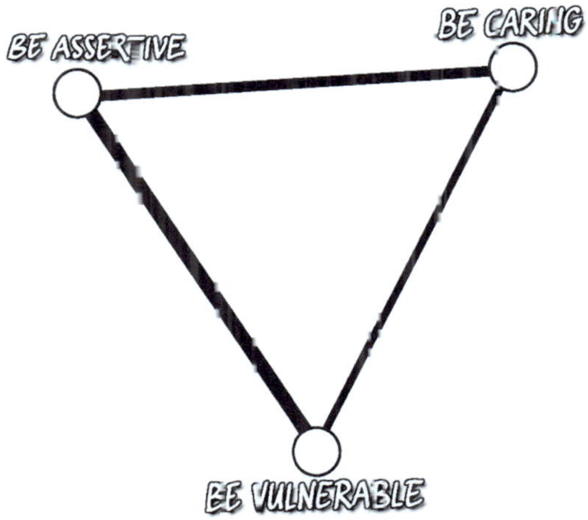

WINDOW 3 PART OF THE SOLUTION?

He was a local celebrity, that dark storyteller who was in his usual place in the dried-up fountain of New York's Washington Square. That day, his fantastic stories were interrupted suddenly by a slightly tipsy passer-by, who wanted to start a fight with him. The spectators, unsure of whether this commotion was a part of the performance, kept watching in amusement. As soon as the fight was about to become physical, two police officers happened to stroll by. It was just about to get really interesting! Will both cops get involved in the fight? The public held its breath, until one of the police officers broke through the public's expectations. He did not get involved in the fight, but instead, he turned to the spectators and shouted: "'You're all part of the show and now the show is over!" The way this police officer reprimanded the spectators in a cool, calm and collected manner, and made them partly responsible, made it clear to everyone around the fountain that it was time to leave. We also left with our tail tucked between our legs…

QUESTIONS

If you open this window to reality, you will see that people sometimes move from the playing field to the stands. How did that happen? Why are they leaving the field? Why is it so appealing to them to become bystanders?

And, what do you, as a manager, do to get them involved in the organisation again?

And, last but not least, how do you prevent yourself from becoming a bystander?

TASK

Can you think of a situation at work that caused you to become a bystander? Or perhaps you are currently a bystander at work? Where, when, what was going on (is going on) and how did you go from being a player to being a bystander? What was the most important reason that led you to the sidelines?

DIRECTION OF THOUGHT 1: PROBLEM OR SOLUTION?

If a problem presents itself in an organisation, you are either a part of the problem or a part of the solution. You cannot not choose! You always have influence and there is no such thing as innocent bystanders. Bystander behaviour is based on the denial of commitments and responsibilities towards others. Today's view of the role of bystanders in the organisation provides insight into your own role and your own influence. The insight into your own role and the realisation that you can exercise influence (again) generates energy for improvements or solutions.

If there is a problem in an organisation, you are either a part of the problem or a part of the solution. You cannot not choose!

The management of a comprehensive school was bothered by "a conflict that had gotten out of hand." The director said: "A small bomb has blown up in the team. Two of us have had a nasty conflict about our new school concept. I am shocked. Just a short while ago, we had evaluated our teamwork very extensively: everyone appeared to be satisfied! Had we been fooling each other"?! There were a couple of members of management present at the meeting with the whole team, and they acted as if the problem didn't have much to do with them. Without words, they pushed their chairs back a metre and communicated that the other colleagues had a degenerate difference of opinion about the desired school development. Bothersome for them, a waste of "our" time and very bad for the school. It is about time that those two colleagues found a solution. The members of management could not (yet) see their own role and their possible influence in this 'show'.

The players have lost sight of their own role and their own influence. The director says: "A bomb has exploded"! That is a sentence without a subject. What does this type of sentence mean? By using the passive form it seems as if the problem happened to them unavoidably. An active sentence would reveal the actor(s) in this mini drama immediately. The contact with the playing field was lost by the director (or in the active self-responsibility variant: the director has stepped off the playing field) and ended up in the stands (in the active variant: he looks for a safe haven as a bystander in the stands). The biggest insider is under the illusion they are an outsider. They are no longer aware of their own role in the play, not realising that stands full of bystanders have a huge impact on what is taking place on the field. The painful but necessary confrontation of bystander behaviour is: "How could you let it get so far"?

DIRECTION OF THOUGHT 2: IN THE STANDS OR ON THE FIELD?

In a team, each member exercises influence on the issues at hand. Each individual contributes in their own unique manner. Everyone is a "part of the show" at all times. Whoever doesn't understand (or no longer understands) this, moves from being a player to being a bystander without realising it. That doesn't mean that their role is over; on the contrary! Bystander behaviour causes or reinforces catastrophes. The following example illustrates the "bystander concept."

There is (in and of itself) healthy conflict taking place within the management team about the desired path. Once it becomes tense, the altercation starts to focus on the 'extremes' of the discussion. The team members with the most opposing points of view start to move around in their chairs. There's nothing wrong with that necessarily until the others (sometimes literally) push their chairs back. They are afraid of the conflict; they no longer ask the right questions that are crucial for maintaining the dialogue; and they no longer contribute to the content of the discussion. They have just changed from active players into bystanders. The conflict (about the content of issues) within the team changes from the moment it becomes an interpersonal confrontation between two opposing sides. The reality is that the other members sustain the 'problem' and even make it worse by their apparent lack of intervention behaviour. The bystanders in this case first stated that they were "getting rather sick of them arguing." Knowing her own role in this conflict – you're all part of the show! – led the director to moan: "I am actually more than sick of myself. I let this happen time and again. I just sit there. I really want to change!" With that in mind, she got back on the playing field! Her self-reflection and intervention formed the first important step towards a culture change, which extended far beyond the management team in the years that followed, thus helping the school further in its task.

TASK

You have indicated above how you became a bystander in a certain situation. Ask yourself the following:

- Are others being blamed? Do you fault others for your own choices?
- Is your case an example of passive or active language use? Did it happen to you (passive form) or are you the subject and the actor in your report?
- What would you have rather done instead of stepping off the playing field? What (inside yourself!) stopped you?
- What did you do that you shouldn't have done and what didn't you do that you should have done?

The biggest part of a group consists of (potential) bystanders. If it is safe enough, everyone can employ their efforts and have maximum effect on the issues at hand. Plenty of opportunity to work together as a team! However, if the climate is unsafe (see Mainstream 1), for example, because a few people dominate the whole team and leave a mark on the group culture, others will hold back. They might retreat and no longer dare (1) to make use of their qualities.

Arguments made by bystanders are often fallacies to not become involved

They might become bystanders for the developing team they form a part of and for which they have responsibility. What they don't realise is that by not intervening, they are silently and unintentionally agreeing to the state of affairs. They might lose their perception of being able to influence the team, their frustration increases, and dropping out and burn-out are lurking nearby.

Bystanders always appear to have plausible arguments. But they are also convenient fallacies to not get involved in other people's business. These fallacies allow you to not take on your role and to stand passively on the sidelines. You can fool yourself into thinking you don't have a role. Examples of bystander slogans are as follows:

- *I don't want to choose sides!*
- *It's too complicated...*
- *I don't know enough about...*
- *The truth probably lies somewhere in the middle...*
- *I don't want to burn myself again on...*
- *My contribution probably won't change much...*
- *It's their own fault that...*
- *I can only see one side of..*
- *It's not worth it to me to...*
- *It's already hard enough...*

If the bystanders change their behaviour and attitude and actively make use of their influence, they can bring a substantial amount of movement into the system they form a part of. The person who has the guts to confront a dominant colleague professionally and sincerely with their verbosity, will bring change to the team meeting. This colleague can even see in the long run that this type of feedback is a form of mercy: finally someone is giving true feedback. Thank you very much! This has ended their pattern.

TASK

- What bystander slogan applies to you sometimes if you look at the situation you described?
- What action is necessary on your part to bid farewell to this slogan?

DIRECTION OF THOUGHT 3: CHANGE OR BE CHANGED?

Learning to understand and accept personal responsibility for your own bystander behaviour is sometimes uncomfortable and painful. It has sometimes been a long and difficult process, whereby a person who was once an active player decided to become a bystander. The (interpretational) questions about what is taking place operate at the deepest level of a person's private life. It takes a lot of courage to allow change in that area. Being able to see your own passive behaviour as a choice you made, makes you partly responsible for the situation subject to the complaint. Blame is a meaningless and impractical term with little perspective in this connection. The manager's role here is that of a supporter: providing people with the courage to resume participation.

Blame is a meaningless and impractical term with little perspective

Theories about attribution show that many people prefer to blame others for their own discomfort and misfortune. It is more comfortable to participate in 'the conspiracy of silence' than to take the initiative to break the silence. We simply don't talk about it, so it doesn't exist! The real confrontation is: "But, if we don't talk about it now, how will the situation be in your management team, your board of directors or in your unit a year from now? How will it be five years from now? And, what will your personal situation be a year from now? And five years from now?" If these questions and thoughts make you worry, there's a lot to be said for participating actively again. How will a bystander be able to see their own influence again? Is it possible for bystanders to actively participate in an existing process that doesn't have your approval and threatens to frustrate you? Can you and do you dare exchange your bystander seat in the stands again for a serious supporting role or even a leading role on the field? These are not easy questions for people who are considering whether the pain of stopping watching is worth the pain that comes with standing on the front lines again. Just like at the theatre, the public around the stage of life is capable of allowing the show to go on, to change it or to stop it. Ultimately, the public decides whether the show goes on or not. There is no show without public. People can shout "boo", throw tomatoes, leave the theatre or applaud and shout "We want more". A person can even choose to play a role in the show. There is always influence; after all, you cannot not have influence. Should you interfere in everything? Anyone who asks themself whether they should interfere, is already involved. The question is what is the best way to be involved and to exercise influence? What is effective?

There is a story about a city that was taken over by foreign rulers. At first the citizens rebelled against the savage rulers, but all protests were beaten down. Years later there was only one ancient man who still walked through the city in protest with his banner. He kept protesting against the unjust and merciless government. The people who saw him walking kept telling him: "Stop that! It won't change the situation." His answer was invariably: "Perhaps I can't change our oppressors, but if I stop protesting they have changed me! And that is the last thing I want."

Taking personal responsibility must not depend on a successful result. If you don't try to change a problem situation, the problem will ultimately change you. Cynical people know this, and it often distresses them. Whoever is ready to step onto the field is willing to pay the price. There is a definition of mental health that states "the courage to do what you think is right, even if it causes discomfort and danger". This is also subject to 'Einstein's law' that states that asking questions yields the best results. The people involved ask themselves again "Where was I, what was I doing, how did I let it get to that point?" These questions belong to the 'difficult questions' category. The purpose of the intervention(s) is to help the other person to see their role as a whole in the organisation so that they can decide which intervention is necessary. Here are the four steps:

Step 1 Notice that there is something the matter

Not all members of the management team from the example were fully aware of the impending argument between the two colleagues. A quick look at the past where they reviewed certain moments from recent meetings opened their eyes. A clear story by both "squabblers" made it clear to the most astonished team member that the time had come to take action. The fact that people don't notice right away that there is something the matter does not mean that the unnoticed problems cannot have a big impact on things.

Step 2 Assess that intervention is necessary

The openness of all parties involved made it clear that the team was putting off a number of issues. They "couldn't get around to" the fundamental conversation about the school concept, the vision of education and guidance for the future. The question "What will the situation be like in five or ten years if nothing happens now?" helps many to see the necessity to recognise the here-and-now intervention. "It can't continue like this any longer! There are colleagues ill at home. Something has to happen. It's high time that I ..."

Step 3 Take personal responsibility

Responsibility is the key word in the bystander concept. Responsibility refers to the ability to respond – not responding is of course also a response. The question that fits here is how did someone let it get so far. You were right there looking at it. Why? Taking personal responsibility does not have to depend on a successful result of the intervention. It's about recognising personal involvement and influence.

Think about the man with the banner.

You were present when the discussion about the mission and vision was being postponed time and again. What did you do? You chose to blame the poor morale mostly on others. You have wasted a lot of time complaining. What are you going to do now?

Step 4 Make a choice or make another intervention

The management team decided on the spot to pull the agenda and to set up a meeting to discuss the school concept. The director examined his role during a number of supervised meetings. The relationship between the two colleagues who 'entered into conflict with each other' was examined in more detail in a number of supervised meetings. The moment the director analysed: "I thought that I was more than sick of your bickering. Today I can add that I am particularly sick of myself. I am going to join in again" made a deep impression.

TASK

- Take a look at your own organisation, at the people who struggle with their role and their need to exercise influence. Ask yourself: what can you do in your role (=behaviour) to invite others to step (back) onto the playing field?
- Try this in the coming week with one of your team mates. Who?

... AND THE ART OF SURFING

The www.alberteinstein.nl site offers you an opportunity to share your own experiences with other readers of this book.

WINDOW 4 CHANGE IS A PROCESS...

Once upon a time there was an old man who lived in an old house by the river, where he was born. One day it started to rain. It rained and rained. The land around the house flooded. After a while, a farmer drove by on a tractor. The farmer called out: "I am here to pick you up before the water rises any further!" But the old man said: "I have lived here my whole life. My God shall take care of me. This is my home. I am staying here." And it rained and rained some more. The water kept rising. The ground floor was covered with one and a half metres of water. A while later, a policeman arrived in a rescue boat: "I am here to save you from drowning. Come with me!" But the old man said again: "I have lived here my whole life. This is my home. My God shall take care of me. I am staying here". And it rained and rained some more. The water had reached the ridge of the roof. An army helicopter flew over. The pilot shouted to the old man to grab the rope so that he could be saved. But the man shouted back: "I have lived here my whole life. This is my home, My God shall take care of me. I am staying here". The helicopter left the disaster area. It rained and rained some more. The old man drowned. When he appeared before God, he complained: "I have honoured you my whole life. Why did you let me drown? Why didn't you save me?" His God answered: "I sent you a farmer with a tractor, a policeman with a boat and a pilot with a helicopter. Why didn't you use the opportunities I gave you?"

QUESTIONS

This window offers a peek into the question of why change processes stagnate so often. It also gives insight into other questions. Do you recognise a pattern in why a desire to change often reaches deadlock? What is often overlooked when implementing change processes? And, as a manager, what can you do to increase the chance that the desire to change will succeed?

TASK

Choose one of the following tasks:

- Imagine an unsatisfactory relationship you have with someone at work.
- Name a relationship at work that stresses you more than you would like.
- Sketch the events of a recent meeting you believe could have been handled a lot better.

If you answer the following questions as factually as possible, you will gain more insight into what keeps happening (the pattern) and what is necessary to implement improvements.

1. The situation: what keeps happening? Who is involved, when, where, why and how?
2. The significance: why don't you have a good feeling about it? What is it about the situation that is difficult for you?
3. The solution: which options do you see for resolving the issue? What other solutions do you see?
4. The skills: what skills are necessary to implement the solution? Do you possess these competencies? What do you think you need to learn or brush up on? Is coaching or training possible and desirable?
5. The strategy: what is your plan now? Who needs to support you in your strategy? What else is desirable to get one step closer to a solution?
6. The result: how motivated are you (be really honest!) to really effect change in this situation? How will it benefit you?

DIRECTION OF THOUGHT 1: BEHAVIOUR IS THE DECISIVE FACTOR

There are no such things as organisations; there are only people who behave! Ultimately, it's not the organisation, on paper, that is decisive, but the behaviour of the people who work there. An organisation doesn't exist as an independent, defined "thing". It's a construction of agreements made by people. As a manager, you deal with people and their behaviour whenever you really want to change something. The more insight you have into the process of change (= people's behaviour), the bigger the chance that something will actually come of it. That insight enables you to better take into consideration the people who will have to carry the change, the infamous support structure. People go through different phases during the process of realising that something has to change on the work floor. Each phase has its opportunities and limitations. It would be better not to skip a step! Change is a process, not an incident.

Ultimately the organisation, on paper, is not the decisive factor, but its people

The fly that tries to fly from the room to the outside is not lacking motivation and effort. It just doesn't see the wide-open window! The concept "discounting" originates from TA. Discounting gives insight into the opportunities, but also into the limitations of change. The discounting phenomenon explains why people sometimes miss possible problems. It shows why people sometimes don't recognise obvious solutions. Or why people, with the best intentions, sometimes do not succeed in implementing solutions.

QUESTIONS

Which meaningful change has recently taken place in your organisation? In what capacity were you involved in creating a support structure in the most recently suggested change? What actions did you launch?

DIRECTION OF THOUGHT 2: WHAT PROBLEM DOES THIS SOLVE?

Discounting is a process in which someone ignores aspects of themself or of others or of the situation they currently find themself in, without realising it.

On 14 July 1789, the day of the attack of the Bastille in Paris, King Louis wrote only one word in his diary on the 16th: "rien" ("nothing"). No one else has ever discounted the morale of the people as poignantly as he had.

Discounting can lead to big tragedies. For the student who discounts the dramatic report, for the manager who plays down the poor mid-year numbers, for the politician who thinks he has an argument for everyone's opinion, for the doctor who doesn't notice that her diagnosis is disconcerting to her patient. As soon as there is awareness of the discounting, it appears to be prudent to play for time. Back to the basics. Ask questions! What's going on? How is that experienced? What are the options? Can we start with that? Etc.! People don't discount things for no reason. All sorts of misconstrued needs and interests also play a role.

If you don't see you have a problem you will put less effort into finding a solution

The questions that many employees raise regarding the desire to become "a more customer-oriented organisation", aren't usually due to unwillingness. Management often underestimates how difficult it is for employees to see the use and need for change suggestions. Employees must be able to recognise the problem (see and experience) in order to make an effort to contribute to the solution. A number of patterns or levels of discounting in a changing organisation are recognised. The management or the board of an organisation that is worried about the customer-orientation of its employees, can receive an earful:

Level 1 Not recognising or not knowing

"Customers? We don't know how customers see our organisation. We don't survey that". "There are complaints from time to time, but we don't keep any files on them." Or: "It's all part of the business that the customers are not satisfied sometimes. It's all part of the system. Citizens always find something to complain about. We just can't please everyone.

That's how it is and that's all I've got to say about it." We don't know the facts at the discount level 1, or we don't recognise that there is a problem that must be handled.

Level 2 Playing down

"It goes without saying that municipalities have to be more customer-oriented. Benchmarks show that we aren't doing such a bad job. It could always be better, but we aren't in such bad shape!"

At discount level 2, we affirm that it's not bad enough yet to do something about it.

Level 3 Not seeing any perspectives

"We should be more customer-oriented, but it will take years to make that a reality". "We have a really nice reception area for the public, but this doesn't make an organisation more customer-friendly, does it?"

At discount level 3 the problem is recognised, but not recognised enough, "because there aren't any real workable solutions."

Level 4 Presentation of incompetence

"We realise that we should, but we will never succeed with the personnel we have."

At discount level 4 we see the whole problem, but we deny that we can do anything about it ("here").

A management team can be perfectly right and still not be able to get ahead. Discounting is an often misunderstood phenomenon. People don't discount others due to "misery." However, discounting of the facts, discounting of the seriousness of the facts, discounting of the possibilities available to do something about a problem and people's own abilities to take it on, is a change process that is too often locked away.

You cannot skip a step!

The following steps are necessary when going through a change process:

Step 1 Recognise the *facts*, recognise the problem to be solved – What is happening?

Step 2 Recognise the *significance* (the seriousness) of the facts or of the problem – How is that a problem?

Step 3 Recognise the *desirability* to do something about the problem – Is it necessary to deal with the problem?

Step 4 Recognise the *possibility* to deal with it – Can I do something about it?

Step 5 Recognise the *capabilities* to handle it successfully – Is there sufficient knowledge, know-how and skills available?

Step 6 Recognise the *commitment* – Is everyone involved enough? Will we go after it?

Skipping a step can lead to loss of willingness and involvement of the people who have to bring about change!

People are willing to change, but they do not want to be changed

Many planners invite others to take the third step, while skipping the first two. "We are going to do it differently" is usually the implicit action plan for the organisational change. The people who will actually implement the change, however, have not been given the time or the room to go through step 1 (Recognising the facts and determining together that there is a problem) and step 2 (Addressing the seriousness of the problem and the necessity to handle it). This is a form of discounting on the part of the initiators. They are discounting the desire and the necessity to involve all the participants in the change plans. People are willing to change, but they do not want to be changed.

DIRECTION OF THOUGHT 3: PASSIVENESS

Discounting leads to passiveness. Passive people don't undertake action, thus they don't make any progress. However, sometimes people are very busy with all sorts of solution-oriented activities but without much result. Everyone seems to get involved in a conflict that has been dragging on (sometimes for years), without a solution in sight. A situation like that is often subject to an abundance of Drama triangle behaviour (See Window 2). Victimising, Persecuting and Bystander behaviour (see Window 3) are all based on forms of discounting.

TASK

Read the following case.

The management team of a large medical institution had just undergone a far-reaching merger. "The negative atmosphere has gone too far, especially in the management meeting", stated a newly appointed department manager. Blaming came up during the different department meetings: many angry and frustrated people, related in their own way that others were to blame for the screwed up atmosphere. "I used to be happy to go to work, but that has been spoilt lately. My motivation has declined to below zero! They can figure it out for themselves!" "The government" will have to pay the price. After all, they forced the merger". "And who has to suffer again?"

What has been discounted in this case and by whom?

Passiveness is a lot more than just doing nothing. Passiveness is also not doing things effectively, and then repeating it. There are four types of behaviour that indicate that someone is discounting something:

Doing nothing

Instead of putting energy into solving problems, the person uses that energy to not have to take action. A person can be very busy with all sorts of things, but not with a possible solution to the problem. They don't define the problem, don't look for solution and don't think logically.

"When his boss asked him if he could finish an urgent report, he stared vacantly in front of him for quite some time; he then sighed deeply and got up to get a fresh cup of coffee."

Over-adaptation

A person who shows over adapted behaviour, acts based on their fantasies about the needs of the other person. They don't put forth any energy into verifying those ideas and ignore their own desires completely. This forms a huge risk for change processes. The person appears to be in favour of the movement, but nothing is further from the truth. They often think they know what others are thinking!

"When her colleague walked past her desk without saying anything, she thought the colleague was angry with her. Thus, she thought it best to stay away from them for the time being. It should blow over eventually."

Agitation

Energy is focused on agitated behaviour instead of actively solving the problem. Examples include nail biting, chain smoking, pulling on hair, doodling, tapping with a pen, sighing conspicuously, pacing and worrying.

There was a large group of employees sitting in the back of the conference room doodling, looking at each other, gazing angrily at their watches and groaning again.

Powerlessness and violence

When a person feels powerless, they somehow make themself incompetent. The energy coming from the anger is directed inwards, often resulting in psychosomatic illness, fainting spells, migraines, hyperventilating, stomach ailments, abnormal heart rhythm or worse.

"She was taken home for the third time for hyperventilation. Everyone felt sorry for her."

Violence is also a form of passive behaviour in the sense that it is an action that is not directed at solving the problem. Energy is focused on all sorts of destructive behaviour.

"When he came home all uptight about what "happened" to him at work, he kicked the dog that had run happily to the door to greet him."

When a person chooses one of these forms of passive behaviour, he often manipulates another person into the Game. By detecting the type of discounting (see Direction of Thought 2) the energy is re-focused on the problem solving skills that everyone possesses.

... AND THE ART OF SURFING

The www.alberteinstein.nl website contains the entire discount matrix as employed by TA to analyse stagnating change and to search for options for effective interventions.

WINDOW 5 SAY WHAT YOU DO AND DO WHAT YOU SAY!

The central heating system was defective. It no longer produced any heat at all. It became colder and colder in the house. The occupants had no choice but to set up an appointment with a technical serviceman. Luckily, he came the same day. The technician looked at the equipment thoughtfully and pressed his ear against it. Then, he banged the side of the equipment. And, sure enough, the equipment started up and the house started to warm up. The owner thanked him and walked him to the door five minutes later. A couple of days later, the bill arrived in the post. Central heating system repairs: €150. The owner was outraged. What was the technician thinking? He was only there for five minutes and all he did was bang on it. And now he has the audacity to send a bill for such a large amount? He called the heating installation company: "I require the specification for this bill"! A detailed bill was delivered by post the next day: "Heating system repairs. Banging the equipment €5. Knowing where to hit it €145".

QUESTIONS

What can you do to increase your employees' sense of responsibility?

How can you view the undesirable results and the unwanted by-products of agreements made? What do you think of the emotions and thoughts the employees transfer onto you from their youth as if you were a sort of parent for them? This window shows how a clear contract helps when making good agreements.

TASK

Think about a recent meeting with an employee or group of employees. An agreement about which you think: "Perhaps that could have been better"! Imagine the agreement clearly in your mind.

- What is your image of what had been agreed?
- What did you do to ensure that everyone (you and the other person) had sufficient opportunity to actually fulfil the terms of the agreement?

- If you think there is a big chance the agreement will not be fulfilled, how will that transpire? What will be the real reason it will not be fulfilled?
- How has the answer to question 3 influenced the agreement?

DIRECTION OF THOUGHT 1: EXPLICIT AND IMPLICIT

Teamwork is based on explicit and implicit agreements: the way people can, must, may and want to deal with each other. Such a set of agreements is called a contract. The word contract comes over as somewhat business-like and sterile initially. However, there is no other word that better describes the mutual responsibility for these agreements. A contract is an agreement between two or more people regarding the type of activity or type of relationship that they have with each other. The most important aspect of teamwork is first making contact with each other. The slogan states: contact always comes before contract. Successful managers are capable of creating a strong bond, contact and contract, with their employees.

Contact always comes before contract

Incorrect or careless contracting leads to all sorts of problems. Missed opportunities in teamwork and failed projects fundamentally have one thing in common: a difference in expectations, for example in terms of the outcome of teamwork or the approach to the project. For this reason there are risks involved in starting something up quickly, often because not all implicit and explicit expectations have been put on the table. Afterwards, that leads to serious noise, bothersome misunderstandings and sometimes, significant conflicts.

Eric Berne differentiated three levels in each contract: procedural, professional and psychological (or hidden) level.

Level 1 The procedural level

This part of the contract consists of all practical matters, such as time, place, duration and resources, etc. This appears to be obvious. However, many decisions are made without explicitly weighing questions such as "Who is going to carry out the decision, when and with whom?" (See level 2) and "What else is necessary to make sure that the decision can actually be carried out?"

Level 2 The professional level

This part of the agreement is where the nature of the agreement is established. What will we do? What will you do? What will I do? This boils down to outcome and tasks.

TASK

You can conclude a contract with others. You can also conclude a contract with yourself. An agreement with yourself about a change or an improvement in your work as a manager can help you to make sure that you will actually realise the change or the improvement.

Contract with yourself

In my way of working I discovered that I: ____________________

I am going to change the following: ____________________

I am going to realise the change by doing the following: ____________________

I am going to do this on: ____________________

The results of this change will be externally noticeable by: ____________________

I might sabotage this change by: ____________________

This change has the following three benefits for me: ____________________

1) ____________________

2) ____________________

3) ____________________

I will reward myself by: ____________________

Signature: ____________________

Name: ____________________ Date: __________

Level 3 The psychological level

Did you have to think a long time about your answer to the question: “Could I sabotage the change by..... if I wanted to?" This question examines the psychological or hidden level in contracts. It boils down to what is not being said. There are often all sorts of expectations when preparing agreements. Ignoring these expectations can result after the fact (!) in: “Oh, I thought you would...” or “I had no idea that you also ...” and “but you knew...” There are two ways that the unspoken, not explicitly made, part of the agreement can influence the progress of the matters: the hidden agenda and something that is called “transfer” (See Direction of Thought 2). The hidden agenda consists of all those, sometimes unrealistic, expectations in terms of what the agreement or the decision will mean. If the professional level is not discussed carefully, the open areas will be filled with fantasies about what should or shall take place.

DIRECTION OF THOUGHT 2: CONFUSION?

We know "transfer" as a term from psychoanalysis, and it is also a common occurrence (See window 8). It simply means that there is no such thing as a completely new relationship: all relationships are coloured by experiences with previous relationships. The strongest effect comes from the most powerful relationship in everyone's life, the relationship with parents or caregivers. This relationship colours almost all new relationships in which you are involved. It sometimes seems like there is confusion in terms of the person, the time and the place; you view the new person as your parents. However, every transfer reaction contains a fundamental truth. And there is no realistic relationship without a smidgen of transfer fantasy.

Here-and-now behaviour is affected by then-and-there experiences

The behaviour in the here-and-now is affected by the there-and-then experiences. Sometimes, employees' behaviour towards their manager is easier to understand if you look at it through the glasses of the past. Continually "re-living" prior relationships brings about all sorts of stereotype patterns in current behaviour. Many managers hardly realise they are the subject of their employees' fantasies. For example, employees say whatever their boss wants to hear, in an attempt to gain control of their own feelings of insecurity. They make agreements that they know will make their boss happy. The vaguer the agreements, the more room they have. If the professional level of the contract is not sufficiently explored, employees fantasise the rest. The outcome is then uncertain and unpredictable, if not inconceivable!

TASK

What contract did you use as a manager to start work?

My contract states:

- What expectations did the employees have at your arrival?
- At the procedural level?
- At the professional level?
- What have you found out about the psychological level?

Ask another person what will happen if your collaboration with each other does not pan out. This will allow you to see a glimpse of their fantasy about your role as a manager.

DIRECTION OF THOUGHT 3: CONTRACTS, CONTRACTS AND MORE CONTRACTS

Directions of Thought 1 and 2 boiled down to the more formal contract between manager and employees on and around the job. However, it is also important to realise that there are contracts in all situations. Most of them are implicit at the psychological level. You mainly see it if an unexpected situation develops in a direction you do not like. At that time, it is a matter of staying alert and knowing how to maintain control of your boundaries.

TASK

Use the information from Directions of Thought 1 and 2 to provide responses that are acceptable to you in the following situations.

- You are packing your suitcases at home. Your holiday starts tomorrow. Your telephone rings. It is your director telling you that it has just been decided to hold an extra board meeting and that your presence is absolutely essential. “Surely you can leave a day later, in the interest of the organisation?”

Your response?

- You have just started your job as a new team leader in the nursing department of a hospital that is new to you. On your fourth day in your new role, a small delegation of employees enters your office. They hesitate, but one of them starts talking and says: “We have a question. What is your opinion of the way management is hiding behind the policies of the government?”

Your response?

- You are in a meeting with one of your employees. A co-manager enters your office and says: “It’s a good thing you are still here. I am glad I found you.”He then goes on to tell you his story.

Your response?

- The porter addresses you as you enter. “Sir, you are always so friendly. Could you help me? The problem is that I was told by the senior member of the team that he isn’t satisfied with me. If only you knew how this man....”

Your response?

... AND THE ART OF SURFING

The www.alberteinstein.nl website contains a printable copy of the “Contract with Yourself.” It’s ready to use!

WINDOW 6 BETWEEN DISTANCE AND PROXIMITY

A manager takes over the task from the predecessor. Upon leaving, the predecessor gives the new manager a piece of advice: "There are three envelopes in the top drawer. If things don't go as well as they should for a while, open envelope 1. If things get even worse, open envelope 2. If you really don't know what to do, look in envelope 3." Full of courage and with this advice the new manager starts work. After the first euphoria surrounding the new manager's arrival, matters appeared to be more difficult than expected. Then the new manager remembers the envelopes. He opens envelope 1 and reads the card inside: "Blame your predecessor". He gratefully takes this advice and the brewing storm dies down but only temporarily. After a while he grabs envelope 2 in despair and reads: "Reorganise the organisation." He makes a plan. Everyone is busy with the plan – cooperatively or thwartingly. It doesn't really help in the long run. Rather desperate now, he takes envelope 3 out of the drawer. He pulls the card out and slowly reads the third and final piece of advice: "Prepare three envelopes".

QUESTIONS

This window makes its entrance in the complex reality in which you manage others. By taking a deep look, you will gain an increasingly clearer picture of the visible and invisible relationship network in which employees participate. How do you position yourself within the organisation? Where do you stand in relationship to your manager? Where do you stand in relationship to your employees? How is the art of bonding in your mind?

TASK

1. Be really honest! Where does your loyalty lie as a manager? With whom do you feel the greatest bond? Whose side are you usually on? Take a look at the triangles below. You are one point of the triangle. Your manager is one of the other points, and the third point is formed by the employees you manage. In your opinion, with whom do you share the shortest line: with your manager or with your employee(s)? Which line is the longest: the line that leads from you to your manager or the line that leads from you to the people you supervise?

Like that

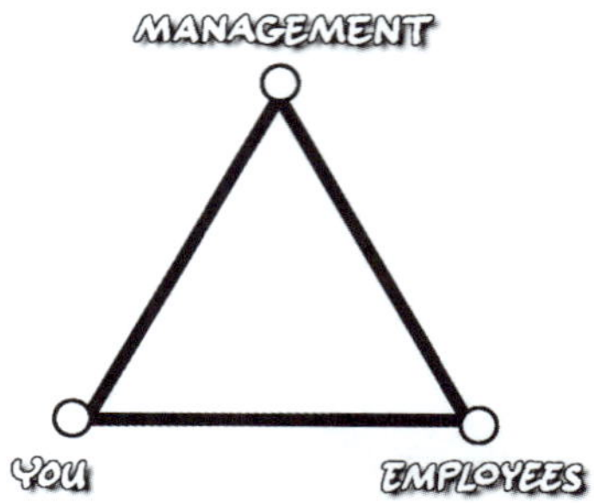

that

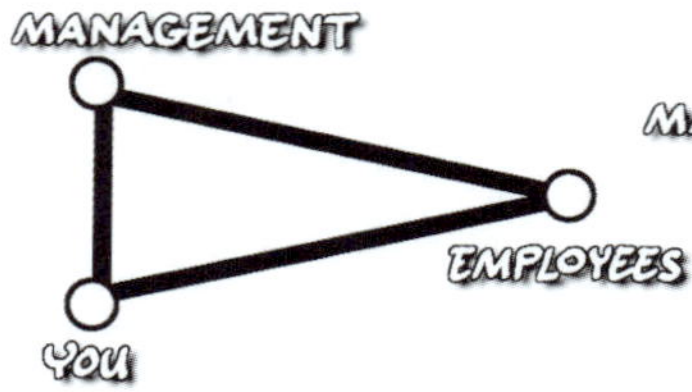

or like that

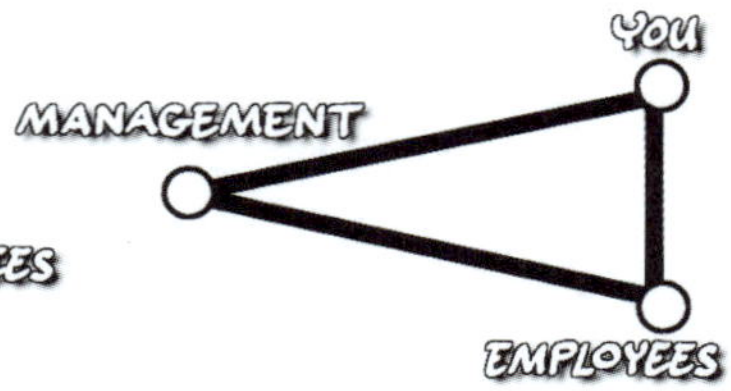

Now draw your own triangle.

2. Does it matter if the distance on one side is longer than on the other? What are the effects of the above triangle? How does it affect you, your manager and your employee(s)?

DIRECTION OF THOUGHT 1: CLARITY FROM TWO SIDES

In many organisations the position of the manager is unclear. This sometimes puts them in an awkward position. You can perform your duties better if it is clear what is expected of you as a manager and what you expect of your employees. Clarity from two sides: a clear contract.

Team leader Petra is just having a "quick" cup of coffee when one of her employees, Fatima, storms into her office, very upset. Fatima says: "Your colleague, Fred Brown, is just dreadful! He gossiped about me behind my back. I don't know what to do". And, after she shares all the gory details about what happened, she finishes with: "Can you please help me"? Petra feels overcome with this. How should she respond? What should she do? If someone is treated so rudely, surely you can expect your team leader to do something about it? But is it all true? Shouldn't she first investigate the matter carefully? Should she discuss this with her colleague? Knowing her colleague Brown, he is probably not so keen on having this type of conversation. It would also be rather difficult for her if someone were to speak to her about her behaviour. Would other team leaders recognise such difficult situations? Should she involve her director perhaps? Where did her responsibility as a team leader lie in this case?

In order to gain insight into the possibility of approaching, speaking to and influencing colleagues, two terms introduced by Fanita English and Nellie Michelt (1975, 1989) are important: the three cornered contract and the psychological distance. The term contract stands for the agreements made between the people in question and for the (explicit and implicit) expectations they have in relationship to their task within the organisation.

In TA terms (See the ego-states in Mirror 2) a contract is an agreement between two parties about a clearly defined plan, method or agreement, which is concluded as the Adult, keeping the Nurturing Parent and the Natural Child in mind. This can be on paper, but it is usually a spontaneous agreement, without a written confirmation.

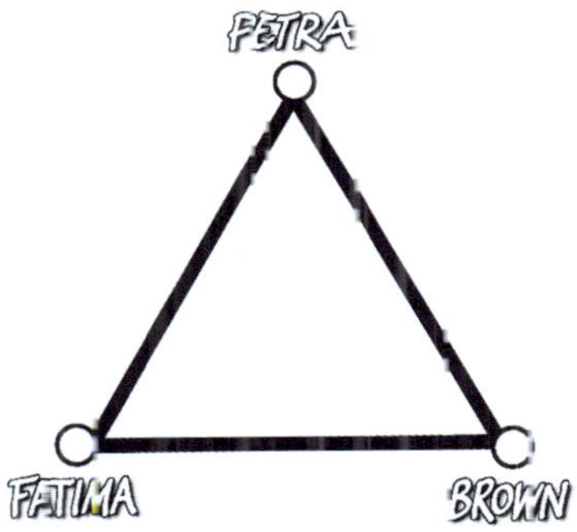

Figure 1

With co-operation between people, there are always (sometimes hidden) agreements about what is and is not expected of a role. And, as Mainstream 3 showed, a role is an idea in your mind. You give form to the idea by being the person you are, facilitated by the organisation for which you work. This type of contract also exists between team leader Petra and her team. There is also one between her and her director. The team members know what they can expect from her: she is responsible for the results of the team, she draws up the plans for the team, leads the team meeting and conducts the progress meetings. Support and control, that is the deal. Conversely, Petra also has expectations of her team members: commitment to the team plan, input into the meetings, providing feedback in a timely manner if they feel there might be a problem performing their tasks. If these agreements and expectations are clear, they have already accomplished a lot. However, more is necessary for optimum efficiency. Petra is still experiencing the tension in the triangle relationship she has with her team member Fatima and with her co-team leader Fred Brown. For this reason, the agreements between team leader(s) and management and between the team members and management are important. The possibilities she has as a team leader to help Fatima, depend on the contract she has with the team members, the contract she has with the colleague, and the contract she has with management. The contract between management and team member is "only" determined in part by the employment agreement. There is still a three cornered contract that constantly requires proper fine-tuning.

DIRECTION OF THOUGHT 2: DISTANCE AND PROXIMITY

The triangle shows how team leader Petra's loyalty is being thrown back and forth between her team leaders, between Fatima, for whom today she carries a special responsibility, and colleague Fred Brown, a team leader whom she works with in middle management. The lines in the triangle indicate the psychological distance that the different parties involved in the contract have towards one another. It is an image of the subjective feeling of distance or proximity which is felt by everyone involved. Fatima perceived that her team leader was close enough in proximity to go to her for help. the meeting itself probably increased the distance in her perception instead of reducing it due to Petra's hesitancy. Petra apparently perceives that there is a big psychological distance between her and her colleague Brown. Too big to be effective! Before significant action becomes possible, she will first have to reduce the distance with Brown. Clear agreements prevent the development of too much distance or too much proximity. The art is to be involved enough, but also to maintain enough distance towards both sides, otherwise you will lose your effectiveness. A good photographer knows when to use a zoom lens and when to use a wide-angle lens. They are skilled at dealing with proximity and distance. At one moment, Petra perceives that she is closer to Fatima than to her colleague Fred. ("If someone is treated so rudely, surely you can expect something from your team leader"!)

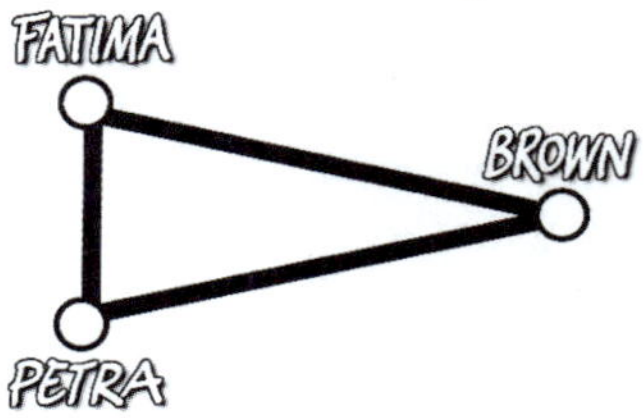

Figure 2

At a different time, Petra perceives that she is closer to her colleague Fred Brown than to her team member Fatima. She would probably find it difficult if someone spoke to her about her behaviour. She identifies with her colleague.

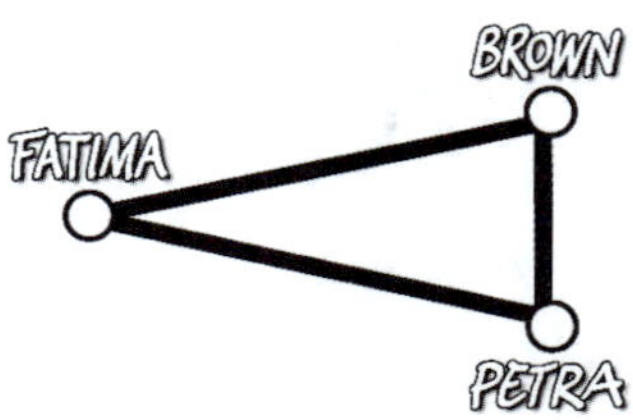

Figure 3

What is effective? Figure 3 makes Petra effective towards her co-team leader. The psychological distance between them is small enough to speak of a workable situation, in which they both can achieve something. The downside is that employee Fatima will perceive her as a team leader who is very close to her co-team leaders and management. This can invoke distrust, caution and "pocket veto" (saying 'yes' and doing 'no') in Fatima. This does not benefit the effectiveness of the teamwork.

In figure 2, the situation is the reverse. "Petra is a great team leader," Fatima tells everyone who wants to listen. "You can really talk to her; she understands you and gives you the feeling she is standing behind you." Colleague Brown views it differently: "Petra? She doesn't do much for me as a co-team leader. In the management team she mainly defends the interests of her team members and doesn't think much of management decisions. Not very loyal if you ask me!" Very effective towards the team members, but less effective towards management. Conclusion: the triangle that is equal on all sides has the best chance for effectiveness.

DIRECTION OF THOUGHT 3: ADVANTAGES OF A CONTRACT

The contract is essential when working in an organisation. It provides insight into what is expected of everyone involved. Even if there is nothing on paper, there is still a contract. There are always agreements about expectations when people work together. Sometimes these agreements are hidden. See also Window 5.

A contract has a number of advantages:

- It is a mutual agreement.
- Minimum expectations are recorded.
- It offers possibilities to hold each other accountable.
- Mutual responsibility ensues.
- Differences in responsibility become visible.
- Work becomes more measurable.

Petra is well aware of such a hidden contract. She knows: "We don't talk about how employees assume their role here"! You cannot cancel this type of hidden contract on one side. It is often anchored deep in the culture of an organisation. An organisation where people openly discuss agreements and expectations, where tasks are established and secured, where people realise that the three cornered contract that is equal on all sides offers the most opportunities for a feasible work situation, is an organisation with a safe working atmosphere.

... AND THE ART OF SURFING

The www.alberteinstein.nl website contains an article to deepen your insight into contracting.

WINDOW 7 BONDING AND DISCIPLINE

Louis van Gaal is a famous football trainer. He has led Ajax Amsterdam, FC Barcelona, AZ Alkmaar, Bayern München and the Dutch National Team. Once a journalist asked him what his big secret was. Van Gaal was in a good mood and wanted to divulge the following (brief and to the point)." Look," he said, "I am not doing things much differently than I used to do as a physical education teacher at the Technical secondary school in Amsterdam. There are two things that I find to be of utmost importance: Bonding and Discipline! You cannot have one without the other. Once the boys understood that I thought they were good, that they were OK, I could really discipline them if necessary. My players also understand that. There can be no discipline if there is no bonding."

QUESTIONS

Communication is a manager's most important tool. This window reveals how professional communication can lead to better results. What can I do to increase the efficiency of conversations and meetings? How can I use the performance evaluation cycle to direct daily work?

TASK

"What did my day look like? When I entered the building, I heard something in the hallway about a dormant conflict that had escalated out of proportion. The manager in question had called in sick. My morning was shot. All telephone calls from that morning were waiting for me neatly on a telephone pad at the beginning of the afternoon. I arrived ill-prepared and too late for the management team meeting. Meanwhile, two employees had requested an emergency meeting with me. I couldn't let them wait until tomorrow, could I?"

Do you recognize this situation? You probably do! What could your story look like based on the same question? Write it out firmly; a little exaggeration can't hurt anything.

DIRECTION OF THOUGHT 1: URGENT OR IMPORTANT?

Everything seems to be just as important as everything else. And everything demands immediate attention and action, with the risk of living other people's expectations and the illusions of the day. The realisation that you can choose and influence how you spend your time becomes irrelevant. Management often tends to develop into this type of incident management! The day is filled with handling urgent matters. The time for important issues disappears to the edge of the day, the evenings and weekends. The important things are, for example, studying possible policy directions, conducting necessary meetings regarding personnel policy and personnel care, fully preparing for crucial meetings, maintaining necessary contact network. Even "extra time" often seems too short.

"Can this be done differently?" is a good question, but the question "Can I do this differently?" (see Mirror 5) is more reflective and provides more opportunities. Many managers experience that the choice from an abundance of tasks is forced by the urgency of things. Important issues disappear into the margins, are ill-prepared and don't have a chance to get off the ground.

Management often tends towards a type of incident management!

Maximum quality can only be delivered once important matters dominate the agenda. The following are crucial for necessary, more effective time management: vision (knowing what you want), reflection (knowing yourself through and through), communication skills (effectively express ideas) and social skills (actually being able to and daring to make contact).

Prioritising based on a clear vision is first and foremost. However, if you cannot (dare not) say "no", time management will remain a problem. How can you lead with purpose, without important issues being overcome by urgent incidents?

DIRECTION OF THOUGHT 2: CONTROLLING INTEREST

Managers have a supporting and controlling role with respect to their employees. Support makes it possible to boost employees so that they can deliver what has been agreed. Control makes it possible to hold employees accountable for their contribution to the quality of the work. To give shape to both aspects, managers and employees meet regularly to discuss the contribution that is expected to be delivered. Individual meetings with colleagues, conducted in a professional manner, are called progress meetings. The purpose of progress meetings is to "make progress." The emphasis is on the light-footedness, the apparent casualness and the obvious "simplicity."

If conducted well (= professional), the effect of progress meetings is higher than the more formal job appraisals. In practice, job appraisals cause all sorts of problems.

Job appraisals:

- Are often experienced as one-sided and controlling
- Often follow a previously determined rigid procedure
- Are conducted twice a year at most
- Increase the risk that the procedure predominates over "what is really important."
- Lead to extensive reports, including discussions about what should and shouldn't be reported
- Give insufficient insight into what is taking place in the daily activities of the organisation.

QUESTIONS

How often do you speak as a manager with all (!) your employees? Do you have a fixed schedule for speaking with them? What are the meetings usually about? Who determines the agenda? What kinds of commitments do you make and how do you record them? How do you follow up to see if the commitments have been accomplished? How does your employee know if you have completed your part?

Many issues can be solved in an atmosphere of trust and collegiality

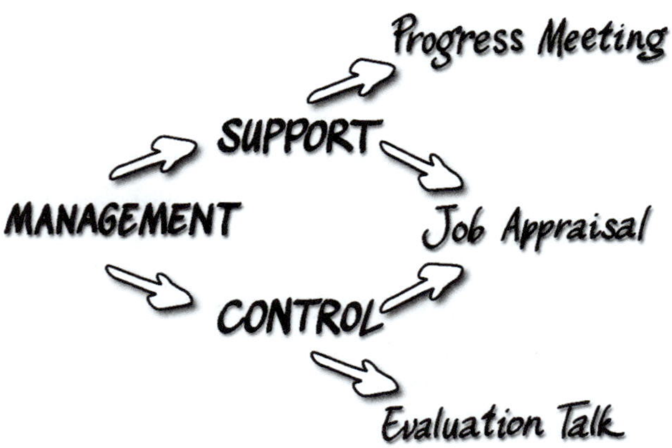

Many issues can be resolved in an atmosphere of trust and collegiality. Manager and employee are generally capable of generating solutions together for all sorts of issues. Trust and confidentiality, collegiality, willingness to work together, based on professional and results-oriented conversation, are the important and necessary ingredients for success. Everyone is responsible for ensuring that these elements occur in the progress meeting.

DIRECTION OF THOUGHT 3: CONTACT COMES BEFORE CONTRACT

Regular contact with employees is desirable, necessary and pleasant:

- The opportunity to provide real support to employees increases. The progress meeting takes place based on a meeting contract. Issues are discussed in a manner that the employee can continue to make progress! The more difficult the task the more important it is for the manager to make a note of it.
- The incident part of the management job is reduced. The structural contact between manager and employee results in a reduction in the number of incidents. Important matters have already been discussed or the employee knows that there will be an opportunity to discuss them soon.
- The quantity and the quality of the necessary management information are increasing. The high incident level of the manager's job can lead to a limited, problem-oriented, and even wrong, image. By meeting with all employees who report to them, the manager has a more balanced and complete picture of the daily routines on the work floor. The nuanced image is helpful for preparing policy and in making policy decisions.
- The opportunities to lead based on the vision and the objectives of the organisation are increasing. The purpose of the progress meeting is for the manager to ask what support the employee needs to make progress. The meeting also offers the opportunity to fulfil the control part of the management job. Based on an annual set of agreements (a "contract"), the manager is better equipped to lead the execution of the policy. That contract includes agreements about the contributions the employee shall make that year and how the organisation will facilitate that. Excellent internal communication is a pillar of good personnel policy. Professional, open and respectful communication contributes to the top quality that each manager wants to deliver.

CONTRACT

You conduct a progress meeting on equal ground with your employee. The meeting has a two-sided character. It is based on a meeting contract. The characteristic of a contract is that it is concluded in mutual agreement. (Also see Window 5). This makes both people responsible for "the what" and "the how" of a conversation. You will establish the following together for a contract:

1. Topic

"What do you want to discuss with me for the next three quarters of an hour? What do you think should be on the agenda for this meeting? I would like to speak with you about ..."

2. Objective
"What should be achieved at the end of our meeting for you to leave with a good feeling? You wish to speak to me about ... (topic). Can you tell me what you hope to achieve with that? Where should this meeting end in your opinion? What would make you happy? In any case, I want to..."

3. Mutual expectations
"Can you tell me what you expect from me exactly? What do you want me to do during this meeting? My expectation of you is that you tell me openly and honestly about ... (topic)"

4. (Boundary) conditions
"We have three quarters of an hour for this progress meeting." And: "I would like to ask you to make a brief list of agreements after the meeting has ended."

Working with a meeting contract helps to reach the heart of what has been discussed. It provides structure and encourages good questions. Afterwards, the content and the quality of the meeting can be evaluated.

Each progress meeting ends with a brief results-oriented report. No long stories, but a concise report that shows the essence of the meeting and the agreements that have been made. The most important objectives of the report are:

Objective 1 Optimum attunement between conversation partners
In communication you cannot prevent conversation partners from having different images of "reality" about what has been discussed and agreed. An accurate description in the report can overcome that.

Objective 2 Clarity about agreements made
Conversations, meetings and consultations – all of this only makes sense for improving the quality of the work if it is fully clear who is to do what, when (and how). Reporting increases the feeling of involvement that change and improvements are something that are continuously being worked on. The report shows concrete action is required constantly by both parties.

Objective 3 Insight into the nature of the issues that are raised
It is handy for both parties to have a summary of the topics that have been discussed. This provides insight into what is actually going on, what is taking place over a longer period of time, and what the resulting solutions are. For management, this is also a tool to form a picture of the subject matter and (possibly) the problems that are considered important by the employees. Insight by management into these trends will logically lead to new policy initiatives.

Professional meetings between managers and employees, leading to results-oriented agreements, form the basis for pushing back incidents to make time for the really important issues. Progress meetings, at all levels of the organisation, can contribute to the realisation that people like to utilise their qualities for the benefit of their organisation.

... AND THE ART OF SURFING

You can find a sample format for a progress meeting report on the website www.alberteinstein.nl. You will also find a "Meeting Contract" card on the website. Print it and put it on the table during each meeting as a reminder!

WINDOW 8 HERE-AND-NOW OR... THEN-AND-THERE?

During a train trip, a businessman is rather rough and arrogant towards a poor elderly man. He does not have a high regard for people who look tattered and he clearly shows it. They both get off at the same stop and the platform appears to be very busy. The crowds are ecstatic about the arrival of one of the biggest philosophers in Europe. To his surprise, the businessman finds out that the person in his train compartment was the philosopher. Only then did he realise his disrespectful behaviour and that he had botched up a once in a lifetime opportunity to speak one-on-one to a famous philosopher. He pushes his way through the crowd to find the elderly man. Once he reaches him, he asks the philosopher to forgive him. The philosopher looks at him and says: "I cannot forgive you. If you want to be forgiven, you will have to find all the poor old people in the world and ask them for their forgiveness."

QUESTIONS

Has anyone ever said something to you like "Don't do that, you're not my father"! Or "My mother had the exact same opinion!"? The other person apparently recognises a communications pattern that they had developed themself in an earlier stage of life. This often came about in the earlier relationship with their father or mother and with other "parents," such as the older sister or the strict neighbour. This is referred to as "transference." One person transfers previous (positive or negative) experiences from the there-and-then to an encounter in the here-and-now. This Window delves into this special phenomenon, in which everyone who manages others should be held accountable. It is important for the interaction between you and your employees to be based on what is taking place here-and-now. What can you do as soon as you become aware of transference relationships with employees? How can you deal with your own counter-transference reactions, which usually help to push communication over the edge into the ditch? It is important to learn to separate matters that have to do with your own history and those that originate from your employee. A comment like "I'm not your father, thank goodness, but you ought to learn to listen better!" can invoke the counter-transference immediately and does not contribute towards adult solutions.

TASK

The following is a strange task, which immediately invokes the transference phenomenon: look for a colleague and stand with your backs to each other. One of you talks about a personal matter to the other, for example, about something happening at home, their choice of studies, their passion for their work. The other only responds by quietly "humming." The storyteller shall soon experience the thoughts, feelings and behaviours that are a part of the transference category. The neutral response of the "hummer" leads the other person to fill in the blank paper with their own ideas and fantasies. These ideas and fantasies originate all too often from "the dungeons of the past." Is that bad? Well not exactly, but be aware of it and make sure it does not burden you or others.

DIRECTION OF THOUGHT 1: OLD HAT?

When she saw on her mobile phone display that her boss had tried to reach her, she hesitated to take the call. She also let his e-mails sit in her inbox for a while before reading and responding to them. "What is wrong with me?" she wondered. She noticed that she jumped every time he talked to her. Well, that man is sometimes very direct. He gave his opinion in no uncertain terms before making sure he had all the information. Is it a good enough reason to react so anxiously? She wasn't a child anymore! It seemed like it was difficult for her to see how the man really was.

It is highly likely that this is a case of transference. Apparently, when communicating with this man, something is recalled, whereby she makes contact with him based on former experiences. Transference often presents itself as a type of resistance.

In a book about transference and counter-transference, the author clearly explains that this is a common occurrence. Transference can be recalled sometimes through recognition of a situation. Transference can also be recalled through resemblance to a person. These are usually childhood responses such as expectations, desires, needs and opinions that were originally connected to and recalled from parents or educators: old hat! The working relationship with the manager is experienced and coloured by experiences from the past. Counter-transference occurs when the manager then responds with their own emotions and associations. For example, by reacting in an irritated or disappointed manner to a suspicious employee. "Oh, he must not like me!" That is more likely something from the past than from the reality of today. We learnt from the American, Anthony Robbins, to view your original family as "the first team you were on." See also Window 1. Our earliest experiences with the dynamics of a team are those we have in the family we grew up in. This first team makes a huge impact on every child. Even later in life! For better or for worse...

One employee grew up as an afterthought in a family with four elder brothers. The conversations at the table were often very intense. She remembered that if she wanted to be heard or seen, she had to bang the table hard with both fists. If she didn't, she ran the risk of being ignored. That was her experience. In the project team she was on, the team members regularly debated seriously with each other and talked excitedly without really listening to each other. She was always inclined to express herself in a very loud manner. This here-and-now situation within the team greatly resembled the then-and-there situation at the table at home. She sometimes flew off the handle. Her colleagues were flabbergasted, but later they were angry with her "when it was that time again." In a number of coaching meetings she discovered this transference pattern. That awareness helped her to develop more options for whenever she was afraid that she would be ignored.

A transference reaction is at odds with a more autonomous reaction. You can recognise three characteristics in autonomous people:

- They have a high level of awareness. They observe well what is going on inside them and around them. They are keen observers.
- Because they are so alert, they possess multiple options for each choice they have to make. After all, they have more facts and a better overview.
- They do not think about who they are in the eyes of others. They don't think much about what others think of them. That makes them authentic!

TASK

A director who just took office wanted to increase the autonomy of the team leaders. When meeting them for the first time the director stated: "You can come to me with all your questions and problems. My door is always open! However, there is one condition. If you come in with your problem, bring along three solutions. Then we will work together to figure out the best option!"

Try this approach as an experiment with a number of your employees. Discuss the experiences with them after a couple of weeks. What is your conclusion?

DIRECTION OF THOUGHT 2: UNDER THE SURFACE...

Some authors state that organisations play an important role in reducing fear or... that organisations themselves are a form of an oath of fear. The founder of TA, Eric Berne, thinks that people are characterised by what he refers to as, structure hunger! He uses the word hunger intentionally. It is about survival, about continuously reducing uncertainty. Structure, procedures, rules and agreements protect people against perceived fear. Fear of complexity and chaos. Organisations assume some of the responsibility for the employees so that they can learn to deal with the fear themselves. What connects employees to organisations is the opportunity to grow professionally and to grow up and become an adult. The only way they can really be of significance to their organisation is if people who have become adults can deal with their feelings of fear!

Managing others does not take place in a vacuum, but in a specific organisational environment. The pressure, culture, unspoken assumptions and emotions about life in the organisation penetrate the process. These processes facilitate or impede the professional and personal development of employees (managers and employees) in the organisation. These unspoken assumptions and emotions are in what Eric Berne referred to as the 'private group structure': there is the visible 'public structure': the organisational chart, the map and the manager who is in charge. Nevertheless, under the surface (in the minds of those involved) there is a different map of the organisation.

That map is the result of all sorts of assumptions and emotions that each person brings to the team in each organisation. We often derive these from 'the first team we were on'. This private structure sometimes impedes groups and organisations from being fully effective. A climate in which people can perform their assigned task effectively is not present. The pattern in organisations that keep struggling with all these transference symptoms (fantasies) can be explained based on the behaviour patterns of individuals in groups, as researched by Wilfred Bion:

- Fight behaviour: fighters react to tense situations with attacks and aggression.
  Modes of behaviour: attacks, aggression, rivalry, mocking, negative emotions dominating.

- Flight behaviour: escapists react to tense situations by removing themselves from the task at hand.
  Modes of behaviour: evading problems, withdrawal, making jokes (morbid humour).

- Pairing: pairers react to tense situations by looking for support from one or more group members to form an emotional subgroup.
  Modes of behaviour: friendly and providing support to a selection of group members.

- Dependency: dependents react to tense situations by leaning on an authority figure in the group, such as the leader or the trainer.
  Modes of behaviour: waiting for support and control from the leader.

- Counter-dependency: counter-dependents react to tense situations through rebellion and defiance from frustrated expectations.
  Modes of behaviour: rebellion, defiance, resistance to authority.

Continuing to examine, like a sort of Einstein, how these interactions affect the roles and relationships in organisations, gives insight and options to provide more effective leadership.

TASK

Allow yourself to conduct a small experiment. Begin the next team meeting by doing nothing for five minutes, keeping silent and looking at your documents. You will observe all the reactions above. Discuss your experiment with the participants. What did all of you learn?

DIRECTION OF THOUGHT 3: HOPEFUL

Transference and counter-transference are terms that were originally developed by Sigmund Freud. He primarily researched the therapeutic relationship between service provider and client. There is always a link between experiences from the past and experiences from today. In our quest for a usable definition of transference for the work of a manager, we came across the following: 'Transference is an experience that is not from the here-and-now, but one that is lived in the here-and-now, which is then attributed to the here-and-now!' Everyone brings then-and-there experiences into the here-and-now. Not a single meeting or a single experience is brand new. The other person you meet for the first time is always somewhat similar to someone you have met before. Transference can be helpful (positive transference) or a hindrance (negative transference). For example, falling in love is a beautiful form of positive transference. Partners who have just fallen in love generally see each other as a perfect match and definitely cannot live without one another! These are strong emotions that appear to originate from the perfect mother-child relationship. These emotions will then change into a more realistic view of the other person. However, transference will never completely disappear from the relationship. Negative transference can cause a lot of pressure and stress in a relationship and can lead to real problems.

One of the most beautiful sentences about the phenomenon transference is by the American psychologist, Richard Erskine. He writes: transference is not controlled by (the need for) repetition, but by the hope that this time ... The employee who goes through life full of suspicion and mistrust can slowly adjust the image of themself, of others and of the world in which they live through the experiences they gain with their trustworthy manager in the here-and-now. The here-and-now keeps offering opportunities to create distance between the past and the future!

TASK

Take a look at who has been a 'beacon of hope' in your professional development and personal growth. Who reacted (often unexpectedly) to a question of yours, to an action of yours, to an intervention of yours in such a way that you grew from it?

... AND THE ART OF SURFING

The Grubb Institute in London offers and sponsors several high quality conferences and courses among which is the conference 'Leading Learning in Organisations - working below the surface'. On their website (www.grubb.org.uk) it says: In a rapidly changing world, effective organisational responses require those who lead and manage to learn fast - and to pass that learning on to others. Highly recommended!

WINDOW 9 THE ORGANISATION'S STORY

A brewery decided to start up an ultra-modern production line. Dignitaries and former employees were invited to attend the opening ceremony. After the formal part, the guests stood around and enjoyed the buffet and conversing with one another. There were three men over in a corner talking about transport and distribution. One of them was the current distribution manager and the other two retired years ago. Together, they represented three generations of distribution management. The current manager complained that his job was becoming more and more stressful, because the company insisted on deliveries to far away places to take place on Mondays and Tuesdays, nearby destinations on Fridays, and all other deliveries on the days in between. "It is so difficult to plan that well with those new cans and the strict requirements by the supermarkets." The other two looked at him in understanding. "That was the same way in my time too," his predecessor said sympathetically. "I always thought it was strange that trucks that came back empty on Monday and Tuesday couldn't be used for deliveries in the area because they had to wait until Friday." The third man also nodded, while he was thinking back and was trying hard to remember what was behind that policy during the time he was just a lad starting out in that line of work. After a while, his face lit up and he said: "I think I know the answer; it had to do with the horses. Petrol was rationed during World War Two, so we were forced to put the trucks in storage and use the horses again. On Monday, the horses were well rested after the weekend, so they were ready for deliveries to far-away places. On Friday, the horses were so tired, they could only handle short distances… Soon after opening the new line, the company changed its delivery policy.

QUESTIONS

Just like a person (see Mirror 6), an organisation also has its own story. A story with a beginning and an end, with a head and a tail. In that story you recognise something about the identity of the organisation. The story contains the hidden answer to the question of what the essence of the organisation is: solid and reliable or sharp and results-oriented or innovative and cutting-edge or... The story can be manly and tough, or it can have feminine traits. What is the passion of the organisation? What is its biggest desire? What does it all boil down to?

This Window is about the organisation's story. What characteristics of your organisation contribute to its success? What deep-down values do you see as the possible drivers behind its great successes? What is your image of the traits in the culture that are more likely to sabotage success than stimulate it? What have you done with it recently? How do you use that knowledge to manage or at least to exercise influence?

TASK

Imagine that your team or organisation is a person. Describe that person! What is that person's story? Is it a man or a woman? Old or young? Large or small? Self-confident or insecure? Why? What are his or her strong and weaker characteristics? What makes this person successful? How does he or she create failure? Sketch a drawing of this person. Or begin the story: once upon a time there was ... (See Direction of Thought 1, the task with your team!). Does your drawing or your story look like your colleague's? Or is it different? That can lead to a fascinating discussion!

DIRECTION OF THOUGHT 1: BEHAVIOUR IS COMMUNICATION

The script concept, as developed in Transactional Analysis, helps to analyse the culture of an organisation. There are many definitions of culture of an organisation. We like to use the powerful definition of the German organisational consultant, Rolf Balling: "The culture of an organisation determines the entirety of customs and behaviours typical for employees in that particular organisation." It is that simple.

behaviour=communication=influence

The good thing about this definition is that it clarifies right away what the culture of an organisation is all about, and that is "behaviour"! And, as you know: the script concept, as expressed by the British educational expert, Trudi Newton, is an ideal tool to explore the term 'culture' in more detail. Newton's words about the script are: "Each one of us creates our own progressive, explanatory story during the first years of our lives. This story helps us to give meaning to the past. It gives us a blueprint for dealing with today's problems. And it predicts the future!" We all write the story of our lives! Organisations also write their story. That story is necessary for the same reasons individuals create their own stories.

An exercise for a team with guts!

Look for the story of your organisation together with your team. Create a short story together! Your shared beginning sentence is: Once upon a time there was a team ...

After the beginning sentence, each team member adds a sentence to the story... You stop after five rounds. You can evaluate this exercise in two ways: you can ask yourself what the method all of you used to create the story says about the culture of the organisation. You can also scrutinise the content of the story. With "the method all of you used" you can ask questions like: Whose story is it mainly? Was there someone in particular who left his or her mark? What did each person do with the slot he or she had? Each time it was your turn, could you have taken the story into different directions? How did you exercise influence with your sentences? With "the content" you can ask questions like: What is this story actually about? What does the main subject appear to be? What can be read between the lines? If this is the subject of the story, what is the story "luckily" not about? Are you successful in coming up with a title for the story together? Finally, can you ask yourself how the responses to all the questions show a part of the story (the script, the culture) of your team or organisation? You can use the Drivers from Mirror 3 and the Stoppers from Mirror 6 for a deeper analysis. How do you come across them in the story? By the way, what makes you happy when you read the story? What do you want to tackle and what will you definitely tackle?

The Brazilian organisational consultant, Rosa Kraus, believes that the organisation's script (its culture, its story) strongly affects individual and collective behaviour. In order to understand that more clearly, you must pay special attention to how organisations deal with four central themes in the daily operations of an organisation:

- Work
- Time
- People
- Money

There is a set of beliefs for each of these themes that pertain to the world and how the world works. We will go through some of these beliefs so that you can ask yourself: how does that operate in my organisation? The four methods can be connected to the four windows on the world. (See Mirror 1).

Work

Roughly, there are four different methods with which you can view the role of work in organisations:

- Work is results-oriented: it boils down to effectiveness, Window: +/+
- Work is task-oriented: it's enough to give it your best! Window: +/-,
- Work is survival-oriented: just maintain the status-quo! Window: -/+,
- Work is failure-oriented: destructive actions, risks, illegal procedures, Window: -/-

Time

Time is a tool that can be used to the organisation's advantage or disadvantage: You can also observe four beliefs about time, based on the four windows on the world.

- Time is a valuable resource!
- Time is a tool to maintain positions of power!
- Time is something to get through!
- Time does not matter at all.

People

Beliefs about people that organisations hold have a big effect on interpersonal relationships, HR policy, management preferred styles, career planning, recruiting and the organisation's climate. Franklin Ernst, the person who devised the quadrant that we describe in Mirror 1, uses short but powerful terms to characterise the view of the people, symbolised by the four windows on the world:

- Window +/+ aimed at: teamwork, respect for one another, openness and trust
- Window +/- aimed at: exploitation, manipulation, lack of trust and personal involvement
- Window -/+ characterised by dependency relationships, lack of influence, poor problem solving skills
- Window -/- characterised by passive and drifting relationships, apathy and disinterest

Money

The view of money within an organisation is a big determining factor in the strategic position an organisation develops. You can only spend money once and money has a huge impact on investments in areas like technology, resources, training and development. You will generally find four types of beliefs about money in organisations:

- Money is a resource to achieve a goal and is not a goal itself! Earning money is the logical outcome of delivering quality!
- Money is a goal itself and not a resource for achieving a goal! Everything is about earning money.
- Money is sometimes a resource to achieve a goal and sometimes the goal itself! Ambiguous: it's just as easy to earn money as it is to lose money.
- Money is neither a tool nor a goal! The future of the organisation is at stake!!

TASK

How do you experience this in your own organisation? Which of the above mentioned descriptions do you recognise? What are you happy about; what are you less happy about? Has your view changed in the past few years? What adjustments are essential? Look for a close colleague to exchange observations with.

DIRECTION OF THOUGHT 2: OBSERVATION PERSPECTIVE

The fly that does its best all evening to get outside through the glass window is not lacking effort. It is working itself to death with little result. However, it is missing...

If you look at an issue in your organisation from a distance, it will be easier for you to see what changes really need to be made, to differentiate between the main issues and the minor ones, to see the foreground and the background of a problem, and to break away from the obvious opinions and initial emotions. But, at the same time, you have to be right in the middle of such an issue, be an important part of it, in order to be able to feel deep down in your bones what it means to work in that company, in this specific context, with its own traditions, with its own story, with all its enjoyable and difficult aspects. It actually all boils down to two perspectives: the perspective of the observer and the field perspective. It is difficult to take on the observation perspective and the field perspective simultaneously.

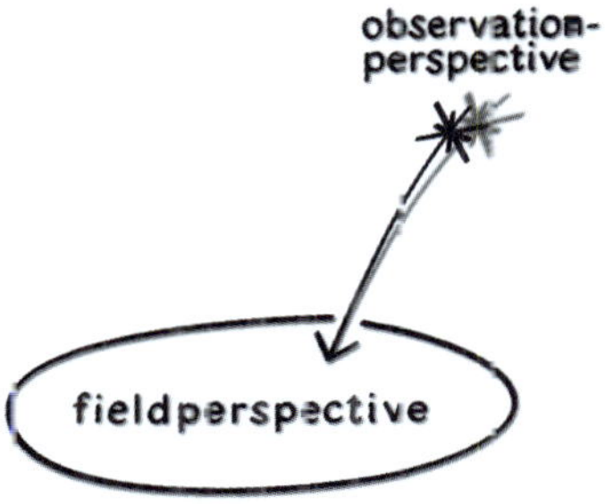

TASK

When you join an organisation, the organisation also joins you. That is what makes it so difficult to look and listen from an observation perspective. Imagine that you entered your organisation for the first time this morning? You look and listen with a fresh pair of eyes and ears. What do you notice? What touches you, either positively or negatively?

People join an organisation, and the organisation joins them too

The big advantage of external consultants is that they are generally fully capable of assuming the observation perspective. However, their limitation is that they can never get a feel for how the system lives and moves from the inside. That is exactly the opposite for the internal people in the organisation. They can feel the beating heart of the company in which they work like no other. The power is in the connection: people who know the company from the inside and the people who see the company from the outside that can no longer be seen "from the inside." A good consultancy firm will want to be a collaborative partner, not just an 'expert' who shows up to tell you how you have to improve and do things differently. It is often the manager who is asked to see matters from both perspectives. This is difficult because you cannot be inside and outside at the same time!

TASK

The time of amazement for new employees in an organisation is about six weeks. When they first arrive they ask themselves in amazement: why are they doing it this way or that way? How is it possible that they don't consider this or that? But after about six weeks, those things that used to amaze them, now seem normal to them. They not only join the organisation, the organisation also joins them. Ask a number of recently hired employees what amazed them during their first days/weeks of employment. How do their answers reflect the culture of the organisation? What surprised you the most while listening to their stories? Idea: give new employees a so-called "six-weeks booklet"! They would use this booklet to note all the "strange" things that strike them: discuss that in the form of a progress meeting and take good note of learnings for yourself!

DIRECTION OF THOUGHT 3: THE OUTSIDE

It wasn't easy to find the entrance to the city hall. It didn't get any better once I went inside. It took a while before I discovered where the reception desk was located. Later on, I discussed with the city clerk what this short search in the architecture has to say about the organisation that is located in the building. He was surprised, but then again he was not. A building gives an organisation or a company a certain identity. A building matches an organisation. There is a reason why an organisation is located in a certain type of building. Often, some thought has gone into choosing a building and often not. The outside represents a part of the inside...

TASK

The next time you get out of your car, the bus or off your bicycle, take a look at the building where your organisation is located with new eyes. What do you notice? Do you think people like going inside? What do you expect to see on the inside now that you are looking at the outside? Does the building exude openness or closedness? How do you see that? Is there a feeling of "come in" or is the opposite true? What aspect of the architecture makes you come to this conclusion? Think about it for a moment. What else do you notice? What would an outsider notice? What meaning can you give to the outside? What conclusion about the identity of the organisation could this visitor come to without realising it?

The area around a building also tells a story. It makes a difference if a building is in the town centre or if a building is located in an industrial area. A company that is located in Silicon Valley takes on the characteristics of that area. Innovation?

EINSTEIN AND THE ART OF SURFING

Log onto www.alberteinstein.nl to find five pictures of buildings related to this Window. You can use them to practice coming up with a hypothesis about the story of the organisation based on what you see.

LITERATURE

SOURCES FOR INTRODUCTION TEXTS*

The story about the art of sailing (page v) has been created based on an idea by Bruce Reed from The Grubb Institute in London.

The story about the old king (page 34) was produced from the hand of Mil Rosseau and was previously published in *TA in Flanders*.

The story about Michelangelo (page 80) is from *Intuïtie en creativiteit* by Marilee Zdenek.

The people rescuer (page 113) is from *Kopstukken* by Godfried Bomans.

We read the old man and the flood (page 129) in *Donkey Bridges for Developmental TA* by Julie Hay.

The strike to the central heating installation (page 136) is from *Principles of Group Treatment* by Eric Berne.

The story about Louis van Gaal (page 146) originated from an interview with him in the Tijdschrift voor Basisvorming.

* The source could not be found for a number of stories and anecdotes in this book. Should an author recognise one of these stories as their property, we are happy and willing to mention the correct source in the next edition.

CONSULTED AND RECOMMENDED LITERATURE

Barrow, G., Bradshaw, E. & T. Newton (2001). *Improving behaviour and raising self-esteem in the classroom - a practical guide to using TA*, London: Fulton Publishers.

Bazalgette, J. (1994). *The Experience of the Family and the Student Role*. London: The Grubb Institute.

Bazalgette, J. (1998). *Leading and managing for effective learning*. London: The Grubb Institute.

Bennett, D. (1976). *TA and the manager*. New York: Amacom.

Berne, E. (1966). *Principles of Group treatment*. New York: Grove Press.

Berne, E. (1967). *Games People Play, the Psychology of Human Relationships*. Middlesex: Penguin Books.

Berne, E. (1963). *The Structure and Dynamics of Organisations and Groups*. New York: Grove Press.

Blanchard, K. & Hersey, P. (1993). *Management of organizational behaviour: utilizing human resources*. New York: Pearson

Bos, A. (1996). *Communicatie in relaties – over de systeem- en communicatietheorie*. Utrecht: Lemma.

Clarkson, P. (1977). *The bystander - an end to innocence in human relationship*. London: Whurr Publishers.

Choi, A. (1991). The winner's triangle. Stroke, 3.

Covey, S.R. (1997). *The seven habits of highly effective leaders*. Amsterdam: Contact.

Dilts, R. (1990). *Changing belief systems with NLP*. Capitola: Meta Publications.

English, F. (1975). *The three cornered contract*. Transactional Analysis Journal, 5:4 383-4

French, R. & Vince, R (Eds.) (1999). *Group relations, management and organization*. Oxford: Oxford University Press.

Goleman, D. (1995). *Emotional intelligence*. New York: Bantam Books.

Harris, T.A. (1969) I'm OK, You're OK. Amsterdam: Ambo.

Hay, J. (2009). *Transactional Analysis for Trainers* 2nd edition. Hertford: Sherwood Publishing

Hay, J. (2009). *Working it Out at Work, Understanding attitudes and building relationships*. 2nd edition. Hertford: Sherwood Publishing.

Jongward, D. (Ed.) (1973). *Everybody wins – Transactional Analysis applied to organisations*. Reading: Addison-Wesley Publishing Company.

Karpman, S. (1968). *Drama triangle – fairy tales and script drama analysis.* Transactional Analysis Bulletin, 7:26 39-43

Krauz, R. (1993). *Organizational scripts.* Transactional Analysis Journal 23:2, 77 - 86

Micholt, N. (1989). *Psychological distance and group culture.* Stroke,1.

Napper, R & Newton, T (2000). *Tactics – Transactional Analysis concepts for all trainers, teachers and tutors, plus insight into collaborative learning strategies.* Ipswich: TA Resources.

Ofman, D (2001) *Core Qualities: A Gateway to Human Resources.* Netherlands: Scriptum

Peters, T & Waterman Jr, R.H. (2004). *In search of excellence - lessons from America's Best-Run companies.* London: Profile books ltd.

Robbins, A. (1986). *Unlimited Power.* New York: Fawcett Columbine.

Steiner, C., (1996) *Scripts People Live.* New York: Grove Press.

van Poelje, S & Steinert, T (Eds.) (1996) *Transactional Analysis in Organizations.* San Francisco: ITAA.

Wagner, A. (1981). *The Transactional manager – how to solve people problems with TA.* London: The Industrial Society.

Woollams, S. & Brown, M(1978). *Transactional Analysis.* Ann Arbor Huron Valley Institute Press.

Related books by the same publisher

Transactional Analysis for Trainers, Julie Hay, 1s McGraw-Hill 1992 and then Sherwood 1996; 2nd edition 2009

1s edition also published in French as *Analyse Transactionnelle et Formation* Desclée de Brouwer 1994

Working it Out at Work - Understanding Attitudes and Building Relationships, Julie Hay, 1st Sherwood 1993, 2nd edition 2009

Ist edition translated into Slovenian, Romanian, Persian and Dutch

Donkey Bridges for Developmental TA : Making transactional analysis memorable and accessible Sherwood 1995

Transformational Mentoring: Creating Developmental Alliances for Changing Organizational Cultures, Julie Hay, McGraw-Hill 1995, Sherwood 1999

Dealing with Difficult People - The Workbook and Tape Set, Julie Hay, Sherwood 1998

Transactional Analysis Introductory Course – Workbook & Tape Set, Julie Hay, Sherwood 2001

Neuro-Linguistic Programming Practitioner Course – Workbook and Tape Set, Julie Hay, Sherwood 2001

Transactional Analysis for Coaches and Mentors, Julie Hay, Sherwood 2009

Transactional Analysis for Consultants, Julie Hay, Sherwood 2009

If you want to learn more about working styles then read the following extract from:

Working It Out At Work – Understanding Attitudes and Building Relationships, 2nd edition

Julie Hay, Sherwood Publishing 2009

CHAPTER 6: WORKING STYLES

Could this be you?

Chris gets through a lot of work, by doing everything very quickly. Chris moves fast, thinks fast, talks fast, and seems to do everything so much more quickly than most people.

However, every so often Chris makes a mistake through rushing so much - and then it takes twice as long to put it right - especially as Chris seems intent on finding a shortcut instead of taking time to work it through again.

Chris also has a bad habit of arriving late at meetings, and of needing to leave early to get to the next meeting! And during the meeting Chris is quite likely to be openly impatient and interrupt a lot, so that people feel pressured and hurried.

Pat, on the other hand, expects to arrive at and leave the meeting on time. Pat brings the correct files and makes sure that proper minutes are kept. Meetings with Pat progress slowly as everything must be considered in great detail.

Pat is meticulous. Laid down procedures are followed to the letter - even when you are begging Pat to make a minor exception. Everything Pat deals with is double checked and even insignificant errors are corrected carefully and painstakingly.

Other staff sometimes complain that Pat is nit-picking, especially when their own mistakes are pointed out. And Pat misses deadlines through taking too long to collect every single piece of information which could be relevant.

Vijay is nearly always willing and helpful; nothing is too much trouble. Vijay can be very pleasant to have around, making sure that everyone on the team is comfortable. Work gets accepted from just about anyone and sometimes Vijay does things without even being asked.

However, this means that Vijay exercises little control over workload or priorities, so that jobs get left undone when someone else needs help. Vijay sometimes gets tired and emotional from being so helpful and complains about being misunderstood.

Vijay also gets very anxious and upset by criticism, even when it is offered constructively. And Vijay has been known to keep quiet instead of pointing out problems - for fear of offending anyone!

Robin is enthusiastic and interested in all aspects of work. Robin is generally the first to volunteer when new tasks are being allocated. In fact, Robin is involved in some way in just about everything that is going on in the department and even outside it when opportunities arise. People tend to ask for Robin's help in their section because they know the answer will be an enthusiastic yes.

However, Robin quickly gets bored with some tasks and this often means that the work never quite gets finished - there always seems to be another important part of the job left to do. It is not uncommon for projects to be handed over to someone else to be completed because Robin's time is taken up with other new work. This sometimes leads other people to complain that they have to pick up work which they feel Robin should have done.

Lee works steadily and produces work at a regular pace. Even when the pressure is on, Lee stays calm and continues to work at the same steady rate. Lee never appears to worry about the workload, and won't be hurried.

Lee seems to ignore how people feel and doesn't understand the need to be flexible to deal with those sudden emergency jobs - everything can just take its turn.

Lee prefers to work alone and never asks for help. Somehow, Lee appears aloof and almost unfriendly - it's as if there are no real feelings there. Sometimes the work is not being done after all; Lee has tidied it away to give an appearance of coping.

WORKING STYLES

These five people have rather extreme versions of five typical working styles. There are many people who have similar characteristics, although most of us have more of a mix of styles. You may not match one of the patterns exactly but you probably recognise aspects of a couple of them that are uncomfortably close to you. Check out your Working Style Questionnaire results or your responses to the following prompts:

Think about what is important to you as you do your work. What aspects keep you energised and motivated?

*Do you enjoy having lots to do, like Chris? Are you usually in a hurry? Can you pull out all the stops when urgent work comes up? This is the **Hurry Up** style.*

*Or are you more like Pat? Do you pride yourself on your accuracy? Does it worry you when you see mistakes? Do you enjoy the challenge of bringing order into the world? In that case, you have a **Be Perfect** style.*

Is your priority to get on well with people? Are you intuitive about how people are feeling? Are you happiest working in a team where everyone's views are taken into account? If you are like Vijay, your style is ***Please People****.*

Are you motivated by almost anything as long as it's new? Do you enjoy most the early stages of each new project or task? Is it a challenge to explore different areas of work? This is the ***Try Hard*** *style, like Robin.*

The fifth style is called ***Be Strong****. If you are like Lee, then you pride yourself on your ability to cope. You may even welcome pressure because it gives you the chance to show how well you can deal with it. You stay calm when there is a crisis.*

In the real world, people don't always fit into the neat categories of a framework like this. However, most of us still fit more into some of the categories than others. We fit even more closely when we are under stress as this seems to emphasise some of our weaknesses.

Alan had the task of responding to a large volume of customer complaints. Alan's manager, David, suspected that the workload was too high for one person to deal with. David was puzzled that Alan's desk always seemed clear but the more he questioned Alan the more insistent Alan was that everything was under control. Offers of help were treated with suspicion, as if Alan thought his job was at risk.

Alan worked longer and longer hours and then he got the 'flu - probably because he was run down through overworking. At that point, David finally discovered that there was a considerable backlog of complaints. Alan had been filing them neatly away to maintain the appearance of coping. Like Lee, Alan was reluctant to admit problems or ask for any help, even though the workload was in fact excessive. Instead he had struggled on. David, for his part, was a bit like Vijay - afraid to confront Alan for fear of hurting his feelings.

Knowing the effect of stress on working styles means you can plan better ways of working with people. You can take care that you do not unintentionally make the situation even more stressful. Had he known about working styles, David could have insisted on monitoring the workload himself. If he'd demanded to see the complaints and the responses, instead of being so afraid of offending Alan, he would have known that more staff should be allocated to this task. As it was, Alan simply got more stressed the further behind he got, and the more stressed he got the more determined he became to prove he could cope on his own.

There are a number of other ways in which understanding more about our working styles can be of use. These styles affect everything we do. They show up in the ways we organise our work, manage our time, how we function alongside others, our contribution to the team, our style of communication, even our sentence patterns. They have an impact whether we are alone or with others. Greater awareness can help us build on the strengths of our style and minimise any problems. We can also develop alternative approaches so that our range of options is increased.

Drivers

As you have read, each working style has a number of benefits. Unfortunately, each style also has drawbacks. These drawbacks are known as drivers, so called because they have a '*driven*', or compulsive, quality when we are under stress. They are subconscious attempts by us to behave in ways that will gain us the recognition we need from others. Drivers are also programmed responses to the messages we carry in our heads from important people in the past. They start the unhelpful miniscript sequences described in Chapter 3.

So a driver is rather like a superstition. When we were little we used to believe that if we avoided the cracks in the pavement, or crossed our fingers when we were afraid, then we would be spared from some awful impending occurrence. In the same way, we operate as if a certain style of behaviour will ward off problems and earn us the respect of others Unfortunately, this is a myth. The reality is that we can never do quite enough of whatever our driver calls for. In seeking to be more and more as we believe we should, we create problems. These in turn lead to us feeling more stressed, so we put even more energy into our driver behaviour, create more difficulties, and get yet more stressed.

On the other hand, our driver characteristics are often the things we did when we were children because they seemed to satisfy the grown-ups. When our stress levels are acceptable, the driver will appear as a strength. It is probable, therefore, that we will be known to others in terms of our working style and how effective it is. If they have a different style, they may wish they were more like us – put them, or us, under pressure, however, and they may see only our negative aspects after all! If they share the same style, they will probably regard us even more highly. Bosses are likely to value subordinates more when there is a good match of working styles.

One important point to note is that drivers occur outside our awareness. We can recognise our working styles when they are described, and even accept that the drivers also occur. However, at the time that we move into the unhelpful aspects of our working styles, we are not conscious of doing so. We believe that we are still operating within the effective band of the style. We need, therefore, to review our behaviour from time to time, especially when we are under stress, so that we can avoid the problems that driver behaviour brings.

Hurry Up

Let's look now at each style in more detail. As you have read, if we have Hurry Up characteristics we work quickly and get a lot done in a short time. Our major strength is the amount that we can achieve. We respond particularly well to short deadlines, and our energy peaks under pressure. We actually seem to enjoy having too many things to do. The saying "If you want something done, give it to a busy person." was probably coined with us in mind.

Our underlying motivation is to do things as quickly as possible. We feel good if we can complete tasks in the shortest possible time. Like organisation and methods specialists, we look for the most efficient way to do work in the hope of shaving even a few minutes off each task. These few minutes can add up to significant time savings across the week. We also spend less time preparing than others do, giving us chance to meet more people and contribute more to the team.

However, give us time to spare and we delay starting until the job becomes urgent – then we start work on it. This can backfire because in our haste we make mistakes. Going back to correct the mistakes takes longer than doing the job right first time, so we may miss the deadlines after all. At the least, the quality of our work may be poor because we have not left enough time to check it over or improve it.

Our urge to save time may be inappropriately applied to everything we do, instead of being reserved for those tasks where it will make a real difference. Our ability to think fast may lead us to appear impatient. We speak rapidly and have a habit of interrupting others. We may even finish their sentences for them, sometimes incorrectly so wasting time. Our body language reflects our impatience through fidgeting, tapping with our fingers or toes, looking at our watch, and perhaps even sighing or yawning ostentatiously.

Our appointments get planned too close together, so we rush from one to another, arriving late and leaving early. We are likely to turn up at a meeting having left the necessary paperwork in our office; we may even fail to arrive because we didn't stop to check the location of the meeting. When we do arrive, others must wait while we are given a summary of what we missed. Our constant rushing may prevent us from really getting to know people, so that we feel like an outsider.

A typical event for a Hurry Up is the time we approach a door that opens towards us, while we are carrying two cups of coffee. Most people would put one cup down, open the door, go through, put the cup down and then return to fetch the second cup. Not a Hurry Up, though. We juggle! Usually it's quicker. Every so often, it's a lot slower because we have to stop to clean up the coffee we spill. (If you never get the coffees, imagine an armful of files to be picked up from the floor, or the pulled muscle from carrying too many bags of groceries in one trip from the car, or the piece of wood that is too short because you didn't check the measurement carefully before you sawed!)

Be Perfect

Be Perfect people are as unlike Hurry Up's as can be. Our motto is: "If a job is worth doing, it's worth doing well". Be Perfect characteristics involve a quest for perfection – no errors, everything must be exactly right, first time. Our major strength is our reputation for producing accurate, reliable work. We check the facts carefully, we prepare thoroughly and we pay attention to the details. Our written work will look good because we aim for perfection in layout as well as content.

This working style means we are well organised because we look ahead and plan how to deal with potential problems. In this way, we are not taken by surprise but have contingency plans ready to put into effect. Our projects run smoothly and efficiently, with effective co-ordination and monitoring of progress.

Unfortunately, we cannot be relied on to produce work on time because we need to check it so carefully for mistakes, and this checking takes time. Because of our concentration on how something looks, we are likely to call for a whole series of relatively minor changes to layouts. Our concern about being seen to be wrong means we are reluctant to issue a draft rather than the final version, so opportunities for incorporating the ideas of others may be lost.

We are also likely to misjudge the level of detail required. We include too much information and have the effect of confusing the recipient. Our reports become lengthy; our sentence patterns also suffer whether we are writing or speaking. We have a tendency (as demonstrated here) to add in extra bits of information in parentheses; not so difficult for the reader (who can always glance at it again) but hard for a listener to follow. We choose our words carefully and may therefore use long, less familiar words or technical terms that others do not understand.

There is a danger that we end up doing everything ourselves because we do not trust others to do it right. We apply our high expectations constantly and fail to recognise when a lower standard would be appropriate and acceptable. This makes us poor delegators and may earn us a reputation for demotivating criticism. On the other hand, when we recognise the errors in our own work we may well feel worthless and not good enough even though others are satisfied with our performance.

The Be Perfect carries the coffees on a tray! The really Be Perfect even has a napkin on the tray to mop up any spills. And they never saw the wood too short; they check the measurements several times with a range of different measuring tapes, find they get different results, and postpone cutting the wood at all while they write to complain to the manufacturers of the measures!

Please People

Please People are the good team members. We enjoy being with other people and show a genuine interest in them. Our aim is to please other people without asking. We work out what they would like and then provide it. This working style means we are nice to have around because we are so understanding and empathic. We use intuition a lot and will notice body language and other signals that others may ignore.

We encourage harmony within the group and work at drawing the team closer together. We are the one most likely to invite the quieter members into the discussion so that their views are shared. This is especially useful when someone is not airing their concerns and might otherwise remain psychologically outside the group. At the same time, we are considerate of others' feelings and will not embarrass or belittle them.

Unfortunately, this style can have serious drawbacks because of our avoidance of the slightest risk of upsetting someone. We may worry so much about earning their approval that we are reluctant to challenge their ideas even when we know they are wrong. We may be so cautious with criticism that our information is ignored. Our own opinions and suggestions are so wrapped around with qualifying words that we seem to lack commitment to them.

We spend a lot of time smiling and nodding at people to indicate our agreement with them. Our own views are presented as questions only, with us ready to back off if they do not like what we are saying. Our facial expression is often questioning, with raised eyebrows and an anxious smile. We may be seen as lacking assertiveness, lacking critical faculties, lacking the courage of our convictions. When criticised by others, we may take it personally and get upset even when the comments are worded constructively.

Because we are reluctant to say no, we let people interrupt us and we are likely to accept work from them instead of concentrating on our own priorities. We hesitate to ask questions because we feel we should somehow know the answer, only to find out later that we've not done it the way they wanted. Our attempts to read people's minds often result only in us feeling misunderstood when they do not like the results.

Please People fetch the coffees frequently. They also open doors for other people who are carrying coffees, even those with only one cup to carry who could open the door themselves. Please People rush to open the door long before you reach it with your coffee - or offer to carry the coffee for you anyway. And they want to know if you approve of the way they are about to saw the wood!

Try Hard

The Try Hard working style is all about the effort put into the task, so we tackle things enthusiastically. Our energy peaks with something new to do. People value our motivation and the way we have of getting things off the ground. We may be popular with colleagues in other sections, and with customers or clients, because of our enthusiastic approach to problem solving. Managers especially appreciate the fact that we often volunteer to take on new tasks.

Because of our interest in anything new and different, we may well be noted for the thorough way in which we follow up on all possibilities. Given a project to undertake, we will identify a whole range of ramifications and implications that should be taken into account. The result is that we pay attention to all aspects of a task, including some that other people may have overlooked. We get a reputation for showing initiative because we go beyond the obvious.

However, we may be more committed to trying than to succeeding. Our initial interest wears off before we finish the task. Managers begin to realise that we are still volunteering for new projects even though we have not completed any of those tasks given to us previously. Our colleagues may come to resent the fact that we do the early, exciting parts of a project but then expect others to finish off the boring, mundane, detailed work.

We may fail to finish also because we spread our interest over too broad a range. Our attention to so many aspects makes the job impossibly large. Even if we complete most of it, we may still think up yet another angle to pursue before we can really agree that the job is done. Thus a small straightforward task may be turned into a major exercise, creating havoc with the time schedule. We miss the deadline or hand in a report full of items that are largely irrelevant. It is as if we are secretly making sure we do not succeed, so that we can just keep on trying.

Our communication with others may be pained and strained, as we frown a lot while we try to follow them. Our own sentences are likely to go off at tangents because we introduce new thoughts just as they come to mind. The listener becomes confused, both around the constantly changing content and about judging whether we have finished speaking. Sometimes we string questions together so the listener has to 'try' and sort out what to respond to. When asked questions, we may well answer a different question – a skill used deliberately by politicians but not so useful when it is outside our awareness.

Try Hards forget they were going to collect coffees because something more interesting occurs on the way. Or they stop to oil the door when they hear it squeaking - so the coffee gets cold. They change their mind about what the wood was for anyway – they may have several half-built items. Or they decide to redesign the saw or build a better workbench. They end up with lots of unused wood with saw marks!

Be Strong

Be Strong people stay calm under pressure. With this working style, we feel energised when we have to cope. Because we are so good at dealing with stressful situations, we are great to have around in a crisis. We are the ones who will keep on thinking logically when others may be panicking. We seem to be able to stay emotionally detached from the situation, enabling us to problem solve around difficult personal issues and to deal efficiently with people who are angry or distressed. We are able to make 'unpleasant' decisions without torturing ourselves with guilt about the effects of those decisions on others.

Because we are so good at staying calm and dealing with all that the job throws at us, we are seen as consistently reliable, steady workers. Our strong sense of duty ensures we will work steadily even at the unpleasant tasks. We get a reputation for being conscientious. As supervisors, we are likely to handle staff firmly and fairly. We will give honest feedback and constructive criticism. We stay even-tempered so that people know what reaction to expect from us.

One problem with this style is that we hate admitting weakness - and we regard any failure to cope as a weakness. So we get overloaded rather than asking others for help. We may disguise our difficulties by "hiding" work away; often our desk looks tidy but correspondence is filed away in a rather large pending tray. We may be highly self-critical about our shortcomings, as well as seeing it as weakness if other people ask for help.

Colleagues may feel uncomfortable about our lack of emotional responses. This may be especially pronounced in those situations where most of us would feel the strain. They may suspect that we are robots rather than human beings. It can be hard to get to know us when we seem to have no feelings. Occasionally, someone with this style will appear to be very jovial and friendly. However, this will be a mask that prevents anyone from getting to know the real person beneath the superficial layer of jokes.

Our communication may reinforce the barriers to getting to know us. We are likely to use passive rather than active voice – "It occurred to me..." rather than "I thought...". We may depersonalise ourselves – "One often does..." rather than "I often do...". Our voice may be monotonous or dispassionate; our face may be expressionless. The observant person will spot that our smile does not extend from our mouth to our eyes. Deep down, we fear that we are unlovable so we avoid asking for anything lest it be refused.

Be Strongs are very matter-of-fact about having coffee. They get coffee when they are thirsty. They carry only one cup because they get it for themselves. This means opening the door is not a problem. Neither is sawing a piece of wood. Be Strongs never have problems - they specialise in coping with anything. If the saw breaks and cuts them, they apply a tourniquet and finish what they were doing before driving themselves to hospital!

A full version of this chapter on working styles can be downloaded at:

http://www.adinternational.com/free_downloads.htm

and click on the link: Working Styles - Chapter 6 Working it Out at Work